ENCOUNTERS WITH THE PAST

ENCOUNTERS WITH THE PAST

how man can experience and relive history

by Peter Moss with Joe Keeton

Sidgwick & Jackson
London

First published in Great Britain in 1979 by Sidgwick & Jackson Ltd

Copyright © Peter Moss, 1979

ISBN 0 283 98548 8

This book was designed and produced by
George Rainbird Limited
36 Park Street
London W1Y 4DE

House Editor: Elizabeth Blair
Picture Researcher: Deborah Pownall
Designer: Walker Pinfold Associates
Indexer: Anthony Raven

Printed and bound by Morrison & Gibb Ltd, Edinburgh
for Sidgwick & Jackson Ltd
    1 Tavistock Chambers
    Bloomsbury Way
    London WC1A 2SG

Contents

Illustration Acknowledgements

By gracious permission of Her Majesty the Queen, page 152
Bettmann Archive, pages 125, 161, 162, 167
Bodleian Library, Oxford, page 141
Courtesy of the Trustees of the British Museum, pages 9, 18, 94, 138, 169
Brown, Picton, Hornby Library, Liverpool, pages 56, 61
Buddhist Society, page 13
Collection Viollet, Paris, page 95
Courtesy of the Historical Society of Pennsylvania, pages 123, 127, 129
Illustrated London News, page 48
Liverpool Daily Post & Echo Ltd, pages 58, 182
Mansell Collection, pages 39, 72, 98, 107
Mary Evans Picture Library, pages 16, 17, 22, 29
Tim Mercer, pages 7, 37, 63, 87, 135, 171
Peter Moss, page 101
Musée de Petit Palais, page 32
University of Reading, Museum of English Rural Life, page 96
National Library of Ireland, pages 65, 67, 68, 71
National Portrait Gallery, page 155
Radio Times Hulton Picture Library, pages 18, 52, 69, 81, 92, 104, 116,
    142, 145, 146, 149, 168, 187
Stephen Shakeshaf, page 172

Prologue

It is the early disturbing moments of a first regression: the subject, an intelligent and articulate woman of twenty-three with a responsible commercial position, has been through all the preliminary stages of hypnosis and now, in the deepest state of all, is told to go back to before her birth to search out a memory in the immensity of time.

For some twenty seconds she remains limp, inert, almost as if she has just died: an almost imperceptible alertness which one cannot quite define

Joe Keeton who has conducted over 8,000 regressions

begins to flow through the passive face and figure as if new life were suffusing through a corpse. Another ten seconds and the slow parting of the subject's lips and a quick flicker of a dampening tongue across them indicate to Joe Keeton, the hypnotherapist, that there may now be answers to his questions, though at first they will probably be uncomprehending and incoherent, as might be expected from a mind awakening into a new personality. There is a tenseness among those who have been present before: who, and where, and when will it be? Will it be yet another dreary recital of a monotonous routine from birth to death, or will this be the exciting breakthrough of which everyone dreams?

Q What is your name? My name is Joe – what *is* yours?
A (*faintly*) Aaaaaaah … ah.
Q Never mind. How old are you?
A (*faintly*) I … am … nigh … my eighteenth … year.
Q My name is Joe: what *is* yours? I would like to know.
A I am the daughter, sire … of … mother Waterhouse.
Q Where do you live?
A (*very softly*) Had … feld.
Q What is your first name? How shall I call you?
A My name … is … Joan.
Q What is the matter, Joan? (*silence*) Why do you stroke your hair like that? (*silence*) Are you married, Joan?
A *No.*
Q Are many boys paying court to you?
A (*a very bitter laugh*)
Q Why do you laugh? (*silence*) Why *do* you laugh? (*silence*) What are you doing at this *very* moment?
A I … am … at … the assizes.
Q At the Assizes? What are you doing there? (*silence*) We will try to help you if we can.
A 'Tis too late. 'Tis my mother, sire.
Q What about your mother, Joan?
A (*subject spits viciously into the room, then sighs deeply*) It is because of her I am here.
Q Of what are you accused?
A (*savagely*) *Witchery.*

For the next twenty minutes with steadily growing terror the subject tells of the trial at Chelmsford Assizes, and gives the year, 1556, correctly, as she does the names of her prosecutor, Gerard, and her fellow accused: she describes the humiliation of 'pricking' to find the witch's mark and of the search for the familiar's nipple. She holds up her hands in abject pity to show the torment she has suffered under interrogation, and finally, tottering on the brink of hysteria she screams, 'I know not Sathan … I know not Sathan … the child Agnes lies … she lies … Agnes lies.'

Her distress is so overwhelming that Keeton quickly brings her back to a waking state and her terrors subside. Even if, as seems most unlikely, the subject had read accounts of the sixteenth-century Essex witch trial and was merely quoting the facts from some strange and hidden memory, there was no doubting that the emotions she was feeling were utterly real. She was actually experiencing in a physical and mental sense the pain, the frustrations, the bitterness and the terrors that must have racked the original Joan Waterhouse four centuries earlier as she approached the most horrible of all deaths.

What exactly are these realities that man encounters when he meets his past? Is he reliving, or re-creating, or in flights of fancy? That the phenomenon we call regression exists there is no doubt: most people, in the

A sixteenth-century woodcut depicting the death of witches by hanging

right circumstances, can talk and behave with a personality that is apparently not their own. They seem to have access to material they do not consciously know in their normal waking state, and conversely are unable to give facts which everyone knows they possess as themselves. But whether all of this springs from supernatural sources, or obeys strictly scientific laws – even if unknown at the present – is a matter of dispute. This book sets out as object-ively as possible the arguments for and against some of the better-known theories that try to explain regression, and then in the case histories that follow, leaves the reader to be his own judge, jury – and perhaps gaoler.

1. The Phenomenon of Regression

Man encounters the past in every moment of the present, but somehow he cannot quite reach out to grasp it with any feeling of reality. Yet the need to be one with what has gone before, and with what is yet to come, seems to be a fundamental part of the human make-up and expresses itself in the theme of immortality that runs in one form or another through most of the world's great religions and philosophies.

For some, immortality is the intensely personal survival of a soul which comes from God, makes a single appearance in a mortal body and then according to its conduct here returns either to the rewards of eternal bliss or to the punishment of torment. For others, the indestructible element is nothing more than the purely physical link backwards to ancestors and forwards to descendants, or even more simply still, the memories of what we were or did being passed on after our deaths.

Between these two extremes, the spiritual and the material, there are a multitude of beliefs: it can be a blind life force or energy which when it has run its course through one body returns to an impersonal pool ready for the next anonymous user. For others still, especially in the East, there is a kind of spiritual recycling in which the essential spirit, moulded by one existence, passes at death to another embryo, perhaps taking with it fragments of experience and memory to help shape the new personality.

However we define immortality – divine spark or the mere handing on of experience in material form – it seems to be the element we are looking at in the phenomenon of regression. At its simplest this can be seen when, under moderate hypnosis, subjects can recall long-forgotten memories of childhood and infancy which appear to have vanished from the conscious mind. And in this state it is not only the images that flood back, but the sounds, the tastes and the emotions, all of which are re-experienced so physically.

Typical of these 'own-life' regressions is that of Sue Atkins, a strong personality in her forties who was told to go back to her first day at school.

Q You *are* five years old. This is your first day at school. Where are you?
A (*long pause, then very firmly*) Standing on the bread for the birds.
Q Why are you standing on that?
A The woman told me not to.
Q So you do it. Who is this woman who told you not to?
A Don't know.
Q Do you like her?
A No – she's big.
Q Well, everyone's big.
A *No* – she's bigger ...

But between calling back your own memories that have been forgotten, and describing memories that you apparently have never had in this lifetime, there is an immense gulf of credibility. Yet there is no disputing that many people who are taken into the deepest state of hypnosis have the profound experience of encountering within themselves a completely new individual who seems to have no connection at all with their present existence. The shadow stranger steps suddenly and uncontrollably out of the past into the clear light of the present with a distinct personality and a definite background – usually a name, a home, a family and a history, even if all these do not emerge immediately. He can describe people, situations and material objects which the subject has certainly never seen consciously, nor as far as can be ascertained, has ever read about.

Temporarily the new character takes over the subject's mind and physical faculties: it hears with his ears; it speaks with his voice, though this may be strangely altered; it uses his muscles for expression, gesture and occasionally such complex skills as writing and sketching. On the surface at least it appears that the body is little more than a passive instrument for an unknown agency but from what combination of past and present, interior and exterior the new personality springs, it is impossible to say.

We can rule out immediately deliberate fraud on the part of a person who is very familiar with an historical character or period and then pretends to produce authentic material in a simulated hypnotic state, as this would deceive no one for more than a few minutes. There are certain very positive indications of deep hypnosis that are difficult to imitate or to maintain, and the information that comes from a genuine subject is presented in such a distinctive way that even an experienced actor would find it difficult to be convincing.

At one extreme there are the 'supernaturalists' who are convinced that reincarnation or some form of communication with the spirits of the dead is involved in regression, and at the other the 'rationalists' who believe that the whole phenomenon springs from material gathered in the subject's own lifetime and is stored in his unconscious until released by hypnosis. Between the two are a number of possibilities, either as explanations on their own or in combination with others, for the possibility of several elements working together cannot be ruled out.

Reincarnation
The idea that the soul or some other life essence passes at the death of one body into another embryo is probably one of the earliest of all spiritual beliefs. The great philosophers of ancient Greece argued endlessly and academically about the details but few denied the principle, and what they called 'transmigration of souls' passed into the mystery religions such as Orphism. From here it became part of the teaching of some Christian sects until it was anathematized by the great Ecumenical Council of Constantinople in AD 553, and so was put at least officially outside the main stream of Christianity. Many Eastern religions and philosophies on the other hand

have never wavered in their implicit belief in some essential element being passed on, not only from human to human, but also from human to animal, and even to plants.

Reincarnation is in many ways an attractive theory both in a general sense and as an explanation for hypnotic regression. It does, for example, present a fairly easily understood kind of immortality here on earth rather than in an abstract Heaven or Hell, and its kharma, the reward-and-punishment

The wheel of life as portrayed in Tibetan art. Regressions such as Ann Dowling's seem to point to reincarnation

principle, seems to offer a logical answer to the injustices of what seems to be undeserved human misery or privilege.

It can too perhaps explain the infant prodigy – a Mozart composing at five – and also the very common experience of *déja-vu*. Almost everyone has come across a scene, a face or a piece of writing which is utterly familiar and yet which he can prove conclusively that he has never seen before. What is more natural than to accept that this belongs to a previous existence and that whatever has been handed on from one body to the next carries with it some memories of the past life.

If we can accept the principle of reincarnation at all, it does offer the simplest and most obvious explanation for the way in which a subject takes on a new personality in regression. In some way, perhaps, the altered state under deep hypnosis releases the memories of an earlier life that are normally buried inaccessibly under the present one.

Attractive though the theory may be there are many serious problems in the way of its complete and unquestioning acceptance. One of the most important of these is the very trivial nature of much of the material produced in regression: for most subjects there is little but unimportant and vague chatter – the colour of a hair ribbon, details of an aimless walk nowhere, accounts of dreary routine. The following extract by a normally very fluent university lecturer, admittedly in the early stages of a first regression, gives some idea of the trite, uncheckable and frustrating material that emerges for so much of the time.

Q Do you know what part of the country you are in?
A No.
Q What time of day is it?
A It's ... after noon.
Q Have you any idea where you are going?
A I think I'm going back from somewhere.
Q Have you any money with you?
A Yes. I sold some things in the market.
Q And where was this market you went to?
A In a town ...

We can accept that in the past the majority of people knew very little of the social, political and constitutional events of the country, and that for most of history the average person's life was a monotonous routine, but even the most humdrum existences have their relative peaks and troughs of emotion. There are so few spontaneous mentions of births, illnesses and deaths; hopes and fears, successes and failures are rare – just small talk and evasive answers of the dullest kind. Memory, even if from another life, should be of stronger stuff, and it is difficult to explain why, if reincarnation is operating, a brownish skirt or a pot of rabbit stew should have some sort of immortality while the names of parents, a home town and a lifelong occupation may leave no imprint at all. But as recall in our present life is so fallible and inconsistent perhaps we should not expect anything like even the feeblest human memory from something that may have crossed the centuries, and become confused by a passage through several births and deaths.

If we accept that reincarnation can be a serious possibility in explaining regression, we are faced with another problem which is central to the issue. Is the new character actually reliving the events of the past as they took place then, or is he re-creating them as they might have been? Can he describe only experiences he had when he was alive and no others? If it did not happen then, can we make it happen now? If he can re-enact only what has already been, where does our questioning fit in? Did the queries we are asking aloud now arise spontaneously as thoughts in the mind of the person then?

Or are we bringing alive, as it were, the figure from the past complete with its own personality and such memories as have persisted, and confronting it with completely new situations, which it acts out in the light of its experiences? Can it answer questions not only about what actually happened to it in some previous existence, but also about how it might have reacted in circumstances which could have occurred, but never did?

Spiritualism

Spiritualism as an answer to the problem of regression has something in common with reincarnation in that it depends on the continuing existence of some personal and conscious part of the human being. But whereas in reincarnation this element is believed to be incorporated in a living person and speaks through him, the spiritualist holds that it now exists in the disembodied world of the dead where it can be approached only through intermediaries, human and spirit.

Is it possible that under deep hypnosis the subject becomes in effect a 'super' medium able to make direct contact with the other side without the need of a spirit guide, and is merely the passive and unrelated mouthpiece of a soul which once had human form? Certainly the dream-like quality of the speech and material of the medium and the subject under regression have much in common, and a traditional seance has many elements which could make self-hypnosis very possible.

Even if we accept spiritualism as a valid phenomenon in itself, many questions remain to be answered in its relation to regression. There is again the problem of triviality – can we place much reliance in a soul which has taken to that far-removed and elevated plane memories of a bowl of watery soup or of crocheting doileys, but none of its bitter lifelong struggle to exist as a body? Or again, are we trying to impose on a spirit world which must be by its nature far beyond our understanding, crude human values and attitudes?

Is a subject's selection of a particular spirit-character purely arbitrary or are there factors governing the choice? The way in which the two seem consistently to have historical, racial and geographical links would appear to indicate that something more than random selection is operating. What kind of confusion is there in that other world when subjects who can produce

Spiritualists believe that a spirit guide can make contact with the other side. Such extraordinary phenomena as tableturning are sometimes involved

several different characters are switched rapidly from one to the other as they often are in Keeton's sessions?

Yet despite the problems and objections there are moments in some regressions when a mediumistic explanation seems the easiest answer.

Cosmic or universal memory

While cosmic memory does appear to offer an answer to some of the questions left unsolved by other explanations of regression, it is a very difficult idea to grasp in purely material terms. The theory is that experiences and actions of all time are stored away in some incredible psychic computer from which knowledge of the past can be drawn if only the right programming can be found. It may be that in deep hypnosis the mind is plugged into these metaphysical circuits and can abstract material from them.

As we can visualize such a concept only by comparing it with computers as we know them today, the whole notion seems quite incomprehensible and no more related to reality than is the distance in miles to the stars a million light years away. But though the human mind can no more understand the universal memory than it can God, there are elements in regressions that seem to form the pattern in which physical computers operate. Questions are, for example, almost always taken absolutely literally. The answer given when Keeton, in an off-guard moment, was talking to an unsophisticated personality from the mid-nineteenth century is typical of many:

Q So you are going to celebrate, are you? Are you going to throw a party?

House of Soraostre of Jupiter from a somnambulistic drawing by Victorien Sardou. These drawings were made while the artist was in a trance

A (*puzzled pause for several seconds, then indignantly*) You *can't throw a PARTY ... You throw THINGS.*

Answers are generally confined to the precise point raised in that question, without any elaboration, much as computers' answers are but perhaps the most impressive of the computer-like qualities is the sense of chronology. Subjects who over a series of regressions have established that that character lived to old age can be switched from five to seventy, back to thirty-six, on to fifty-three and then to ten, and will begin the story instantly at that year without producing a single fact that the personality would not have known at that precise time. Sometimes they are given a definite date, sometimes a specific age, but in either case the material begins immediately, without that momentary pause that even mathematical minds need to make the mental calculations. A subject who is talking excitedly about a person or place at twenty-one may well deny all knowledge of the name a second later when taken to eighteen if in his other existence he had not known them at that age.

Even more dramatically, subjects who have established several personalities can be rushed from one to the other very rapidly and never have the slightest confusion in subject matter or accent relating to each character. To complicate the situation even further they can be moved not only to different personalities, but also to different ages in those personalities all in the space of a single session, and so far not one subject has faltered for a moment.

Ancestral or genetic memory

There appears to be a strong geographical element in regression, and subjects in England so far have always returned to a personality somewhere in the British Isles, often within a relatively short distance of where they now live. A sceptic might suggest that staying close to home gives the mind – quite unconsciously – a better chance of getting more of the background material right than if it appeared in a distant and unfamiliar country or setting. It could also, of course, indicate that at least some of the facts have been handed on genetically as a high proportion of the people of Britain still remain fairly close to where their families have always lived, and though it is often difficult to establish a direct blood line much before the mid-nineteenth century, it becomes much more likely within a small area.

No one denies that physical qualities are handed on: can it be that memory is also passed on and is a factor in regression – it could account for some of the confusion subjects often experience with their material. While it is fairly easy to sort out and allocate a person's physical characteristics, it would be extremely difficult for a subject under hypnosis to disentangle the vague memories that float in from a whole line of ancestors.

It is difficult to quote any piece of regression dialogue which seems to

(left) Emperor Maximilian I (1459–1519) (right) Emperor Ferdinand I (1793–1875). The famous Habsburg chin and nose are still clearly visible in the photograph of Ferdinand even though he was born over two centuries later than Maximilian

point directly to hereditary memory as the source of the information because if there is a long interval between the lives of the subject and his personality it is often impossible to establish a definite link. If there is only a short period between the two generations, there is a suspicion that the recollections may have been transmitted, quite unconsciously, by nothing more mysterious than human tongues and ears. Perhaps a small child, long before it can speak, overhears parents and grandparents talking over family history. Quite unaware of what is being said, the child could absorb the information and in later life as an adult could regress, bringing out from his unconscious the details of two hundred years before.

There are other even more important considerations that must be examined before accepting hereditary memory as the total explanation of regression. The passing on of any characteristics, physical or psychic, does depend on having children, and a high proportion of subjects 'die' in infancy or for some other reason have no family. Of the seven personalities that are considered in this book, only four claimed to have children.

Another serious problem is that most subjects can describe their 'death'. If memory can be transmitted genetically from parents to children it would be reasonable to assume that nothing could be added to the store after conception – that is, family recollections would cease at some age when the mother was generally under forty. And this is just not true.

Perhaps we are examining the whole process in terms of normal laws of physical heredity, which may not apply any more than if we expected mind always to obey the same laws as muscle.

Telepathy

With telepathy we are moving into an area where there does seem to be definite scientific evidence that the phenomenon exists, but what part if any it plays in helping a subject under hypnosis to produce accurate facts needs a great deal more investigation.

Most of us are familiar with what seems to be a simple form of telepathy in everyday life: two people begin to speak the same word or to hum the same tune simultaneously without any outside suggestion or prompting, or a person walking along a street is suddenly aware of being watched, and turning round finds that a complete stranger fifty metres away is staring at him. In neither case is there any physical contact, yet some part of the mind responds as positively and as actively as if there had been a shout, a touch or a visual signal.

With professional sensitives working under laboratory conditions all over the world results are even more remarkable, and although there seems fairly reliable proof that images, words and sensations can be transmitted, no one can yet explain precisely what is happening.

Before we can even guess if and how telepathy is relevant to regression we need to know much more about telepathy itself. Is it possible, for example, for one person to probe the mind of another who is purely passive and quite unaware that the facts are being sought, and found, in his mind?

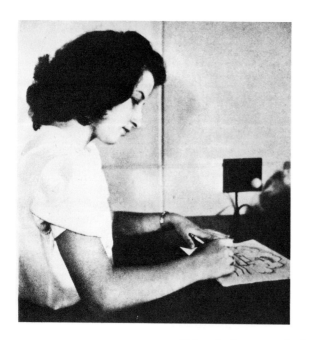

Telepathy is a recognized, if little understood, phenomenon. One twin tries to reproduce a picture at which her sister is looking in another room

Does the sender actually need to be thinking of the information at the time, or need it be in his conscious mind at all? Can the person seeking the material tune in, quite unconsciously, to another mind as he might flick across the dial of a radio at random until he hears the kind of music he wants, completely unaware of the station that is sending it out?

From observation it seems unlikely that a subject deliberately seeks information outside himself, but poses the question to that part of his mind which is operating, and receives a reply through what are apparently his own normal thought processes. Even the conscious mind that has been observing the whole exchange is quite unaware that telepathy has been involved – if indeed it has.

Telepathy is an unfortunate factor to have to take into consideration because even if it is not operating, there is always the suspicion that it might be. It is particularly dangerous when a subject regresses to a known historical character because with perhaps ten observers present a fairly comprehensive mental biography can be built up. If in some way this material becomes available to the person under hypnosis then there is the possibility that we are observing an incredibly fascinating experience, but not what we generally mean by regression to the past.

Edna Greenan, whose full story is given later, 'becomes' Nell Gwynn, the seventeenth-century actress, courtesan and mistress of Charles II. The real Nell had two sons by the King, one of whom died in infancy and another who became the Duke of St Albans. In this sequence she had been taken to her late twenties and was being questioned by someone who had done some detailed research on the Restoration court.

Q Does he [i.e. her son] go to school, Nell?
A (*pause*) To learn his letters do you mean?
Q Yes.
A He goes to t'palace.
Q Do you know who he learns his letters from? (*silence*) Try hard, Nelly.
A (*confidently*) Orrery.
Q Orrery?
A (*still confident*) Orrery. (*slightly hesitant*) Orrery ... (*doubtful*) Or ... Orr ... ery.
Q Is it?
A (*meditatively*) Orrery. He's written something and the people don't like him because they say he's always in his cups.

Nell Gwynn's son was taught by Thomas Otway and not by his fellow court dramatist, Roger Orrery. It could be that the subject, groping in the blackness for the answer to this very obscure question, picked up telepathically the initial 'O' together with some association with the theatre from the observer who knew well enough that the name was Otway, but could find nothing except the word Orrery to relate with it. It is known that the historical Nell Gwynn acted in at least two plays by Roger Orrery, but almost certainly none by Otway.

As so often when trying to find out what is happening in regression, just as it seems that at last a definite factor has been identified, the whole theory collapses. For every session (like Edna Greenan's) in which telepathy does seem to be significant, there are two when it appears to be a definite hindrance. A character may be asked a simple question – a well-to-do woman in the 1890s told to say who was on the throne, for example – the answer to which everyone in the room knows. Every mind automatically and silently shouts out the word 'Victoria', willing the reply, but this seems only to drive the subject into doltish 'Don't knows', though it is obvious that the person being regressed knows the answer as herself and would certainly have known it as the other personality.

Perhaps in the end telepathy under hypnosis is just as variable as it is in the waking state: it would be interesting to find out whether people who have the ability to transmit and receive thought in everyday life can still do so under hypnosis, or whether the process of being hypnotized releases the power from the hidden mind.

The unconscious
It could be that there is nothing supernatural at all about regression, and the apparent ability to reach out into the past to find an earlier existence is nothing more than an unbelievably complex functioning of the mind working on material it has accumulated quite normally in the subject's present lifetime.

Most psychologists agree that there are two main elements in what we call the mind – the conscious and the unconscious. The conscious is that function of the brain that takes in the countless billions of pieces of information that pour into the senses whether we are awake or asleep; it stores, indexes and cross-references them and produces the data needed to make the continuous stream of decisions that shape our life. The conscious mind can remember, relate one experience with another, analyse and predict: whether we merely raise an arm or work out an abstract philosophical theory it is this great resevoir of knowledge that is recalled to direct the operation.

But this part of the mind seems capable of handling only a minute fraction of the material that has battered it from the eyes, ears, skin, tongue and nose twenty-four hours a day from birth. By far the greater part is apparently too trivial or too irrevelant to the individual's daily life to be stored where it can be recalled at will, and may pass direct to the deeper layers. Here it may be joined by material which we once knew but have forgotten – really forgotten that is, so that no matter how much we are reminded or prompted we cannot recall it. From time to time too, a traumatic experience such as violence, sorrow or fear is thought to be too terrible or too damaging for the conscious to retain, and that, as well as the trivia, vanishes into the limbo of the unconscious.

If I walk along a street my conscious at the end may recall only the title of the new thriller I saw in the bookshop and the frantic squeal of brakes at the

Spirit drawing by Frederika Bremer tries to capture elements of the unconscious

pedestrian crossing: my unconscious on the other hand has perhaps filed away not only the titles, authors, prices and jacket details of every book in the window; the colour, make, model, registration number of the car and complete descriptions of all the occupants, but also the number of lampposts, windows, doors, and full details of every poster, pedestrian and vehicle.

In a similar way scenes we saw as small children being taken by car or train to places we are not aware we have ever visited; characters and plots from ephemeral books we read at school and whose titles and authors we would in all honesty deny we have ever known; photographs of people and places and things we have glanced at with unseeing eyes in forgotten waiting rooms; snatches of speech from radio programmes of our youth, from strangers on buses and in crowds, from sermons and from acquaintances we have not seen for forty years; they are all, perhaps, timed, filed and catalogued in some deep repository of the mind.

Unfortunately we have virtually no idea at all what is really happening in these deeper layers of the mind because the only instrument we can use to examine them is the mind itself. As Carl Jung, the great psychologist who did so much work on the unconscious, said: '… the very act of observing alters the observed. Consequently there is at present no way of objectively determining the real nature of the unconscious.'

Is it the unconscious memory we are listening to in this remarkable sequence from a regression by a Methodist minister, at present working in Washington, but originally from Edmond, Oklahoma. He had become 'Petros' from an unidentified place in Europe named Schweinberg, and although the date was never established, the context seemed to indicate the twelfth to thirteenth centuries. Petros said that he was nineteen and was studying alchemy under Old Schlaak.

Q Where are you at this moment?
A In my room.
Q Have you any equipment there to work on?
A (*pause*) A … candle.
Q Anything else?
A Two books.
Q What are they called?
A (*long silence then*) I can see the writing in them.
Q Can you read me some? (*look of intense concentration, but no sound*) Look hard … try to read just one word.
A (*silence. Subject vaguely lifts up hands as if they had a large book in them, leans forward to peer at the invisible volume. He then shifts his grip so that the 'book' is held across the spine by the left hand only, while the index finger of the right points as if to a word. The finger then traces slowly across the 'page' from right to left, jerking forward at each syllable. But there is no sound*)
Q Can you spell it out?
A (*as if suddenly making sense of the letters*) Ad … regnum … div … diviso … est … est … sui … (*the index finger moves back to the beginning of the same line*

as if the personality now comprehended) Ad regnum divisus, sui ...
Q Can you read these words again loudly?
A (*angrily*) *I've read them.* Sui ... genera ...
Q Sui genera – what is after 'sui genera'?
A (*long pause of concentration*) Qui ... qui ... qui ... con ... constab ...
    constabu ... (*triumphantly*) *Constabulariis.*

The minister said that although he had studied Hebrew and could understand a little classical Greek, he had no Latin – attempted it for one term at
school and then abandoned it. He was adamant that the book he had been
'reading' was written in Hebrew – which would be in keeping with the
right-to-left sequence – and he thought that he had been speaking in that
language instead of the Latin that emerged.

The words make little sense, but if we make allowances for serious gram-
matical errors the words could mean 'To the divided kingdom ... is ... one
who is set apart, unique ... who ...' 'Constabulariis' which was brought out
with such difficulty is probably a confusion with another word – unless it is
the late Latin 'comes stabuli', count, or lord of the stable. Is this an unconscious memory of those few weeks of Latin so many years ago? The
actual words do not look like those from a classical primer, but they could
well be something from an uncomprehending glance at a copy of the
Vulgate or an old devotional book seen in the course of study at college.
The feeling that this may be unconscious memory is strengthened by the
personality's choice of name, Petros – the Greek for Peter – as this is normally associated with the apostle.

Is regression no more than a mosaic of controlled dreaming from our
unconscious minds rather than something from before our birth? Are we
taking as a basic framework one of the many facets of our personality and
clothing it with the rich unknown material stored in the deepest layers of
the mind? Does a woman, perhaps quite unwittingly, give rein to the
masculine element in herself and under regression become a man, or is the
quiet 'mouse' living a dull routine life released for an hour to strut involuntarily as a loud, swashbuckling extrovert?

While some evidence does seem to point in this direction there are the
inevitable difficulties, the most serious of which is how even the unconscious can ever have had access to some pieces of information which are
recorded only in obscure and inaccessible places that take weeks of research
to uncover. Where would an ordinary housewife learn that in the 1840s an
observatory at Liverpool agreed to synchronize its chronometers with
those at Greenwich, which meant 'losing' forty-eight seconds? How did
another find out the subtitles of plays by the seventeenth-century dramatists
Dryden and Heywood and reject the main titles when they were put to her?

While an explanation of at least part of regression in terms of material
gathered in the present life may disappoint those who long for a mystical
solution, the incredible complexity of the mind that it reveals makes, if
anything, the natural more wonderful than the supernatural.

2. The Experience of Regression

For many people hypnosis unfortunately has sinister overtones even if there is a frightened fascination as well, so that in any new regression group there is always that strange mixture of excitement and apprehension that marks any contact with the unknown. Newcomers talk quickly and nervously to cover the tension; cigarettes and coffee vanish rapidly, and then slowly the comforting, inconsequential chatter narrows down to the matter on every-one's mind – what exactly hypnosis is.

It is certainly not sleep in the accepted sense, for although the eyes are usually lightly closed, the waking, reasoning mind is fully conscious and totally aware of the surroundings. The subject can hear everything that is happening in the room, but more importantly he can listen critically, even if helplessly, to the voice of the body of which he no longer seems part. On being brought back, too, his conscious mind has a dual set of memories – everything that happened in the room during hypnosis, and also all that the other mind did and said and thought. The images of people and places and events, and all the emotions it felt, remain as part of the new memories just as real as if they had been experienced by the physical body.

That hypnosis is not normal sleep is positively confirmed by examining the brain waves of subjects on the electroencephalograph – one of the very few objective scientific tests that can be applied at present. The brain of a person who is wide awake but sitting quietly with his eyes closed emits the rapid and regular alpha waves shown in (1); as he becomes drowsy these change to the irregular pattern (2); and when he finally falls asleep the rhythm becomes slower and larger as at (3). Even in the very deepest hypnotic state the brain stubbornly refuses to show anything but the normal waking alpha form.

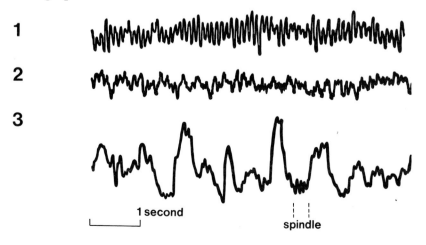

To watch Keeton at work it seems an incredibly simple process, even if the reality is very different. There is no darkened room, full of incense and dim shadows, beloved of novelists and scriptwriters: no staring at shining pendulums or flickering flames; no stylized gestures in the air or passes across the forehead; no tinkling bells or the faint slow beat of percussion; no Svengali-type glare; nothing but an ordinary room in an ordinary house lit by ordinary lighting, either the sun or electricity. And all the while the voice of the hypnotist quietly but firmly insists on total commitment and complete trust on the part of the subject.

Keeton talks steadily and persuasively of sleep; of the enfolding rest of relaxation; of the mental abilities that are man's heritage but which he has lost on his long evolutionary journey, just as he has lost the power to use some muscle groups. He suggests the deep, rich, black softness of velvet wrapping round, shutting out the world, and then in the monotone which is not a monotone tells the subject not to close his eyes until compulsion presses them shut.

And all the while the frequency of his speech slowly and imperceptibly drifts, hunting, hunting until it matches the subject's natural brain rhythms. He can detect instantly when voice and mind are beating in unison and locks at this speed: usually within a few seconds the eyelids droop … are forced back … and droop again as Keeton suggests there are weights being placed on them. There are a few spasmodic flickers, and the eyes close in the lightest hypnotic state. The voice beats on, deep, rhythmic, slow, taking the subject deeper and deeper into a relaxed state and the subject visibly relaxes. When he judges the trance to be deep enough Joe Keeton gives subjects a codeword to which they will respond at any time, and then wakens them. In the animated conversation that follows, Keeton will quite unexpectedly and out of context quietly let slip the code words: they pass almost unnoticed by most of the group until the subject, if still seated, gives a deep sigh and falls back on the chair with closing eyes. He is taken deeper still and told to go back in time to some point in childhood – usually the first day at school as this tends to leave indelible marks of one kind or another in most people.

This is a danger here, because there are few who with their ordinary conscious mind could not give some details of the occasion, and Keeton watches carefully for the signs that the subject is actually reliving the experience – the spontaneous use of the present tense, for example, in such sentences as 'Teacher IS telling us to hang up our coats …' rather than the expected 'Teacher TOLD us …'

If this is successful, the subject is generally taken to the age of three or even earlier, before being brought awake, when he will almost certainly comment on the vividness of the experience: 'I really felt it when Charlie thumped me …' or 'I was terrified when my mum left me … I could feel my heart pounding …' Usually a subject is not taken any further in a first session, but at this stage there is no shortage of volunteers.

What has been described is, of course, an ideal situation achieved by no more than one or two people in every dozen at a first attempt. Some cannot be hypnotized at all, possibly because of fears they cannot overcome deep inside, however much the conscious may wish it; some can be hypnotized only lightly; others who can be put into a deeply relaxed state cannot be taken back to their earlier days perhaps because of some unhappy experience repressed into the unconscious.

An interval of at least a day is generally left between returning to the early days of one's own life, and searching for a memory in the immensity of all time. This is the moment when credulity is stretched to the limit, and the faint-hearted return in disbelief or fear to the security of the mechanical world of substance.

The subject is encouraged deeper and deeper into relaxation, and to put an even greater trust in the hypnotist, who holds the lifeline if, as so often happens, a terrifying experience occurs. It is possible that on the initial journey back, groping through the ages, the first incident that leaps from the darkness of the unknown is the most horrible of all existences. Typical of the first moments of a regression to before birth is the following by Sue Atkins:

Q Where are you? (*repeated several times with no response apart from a faint physical stirring*) *Where are you?*
A (*very faintly*) Aaaaaaaaaa.
Q What's the matter?
A (*very deep sigh*)
Q What's the matter?
A (*faintly*) Aaaah.
Q What's your name?
A Aah.
Q (*more insistently*) *What is your name?*
A (*louder – the tension and terror in the voice is obvious*) AAAAAH.
Q Are you ill?
A (*sharply, pathetically*) *AAH ... AH.*
Q Do you understand us?
A (*much louder still*) *AAAAAAH.*
Q Are you ill?
A (*shouting, terrified*) *AAAAH ... AAAAAAAAAH.* (*pause, then very faintly, only just audible*) Fire ... (*a little louder*) Fire. (*pause, then louder still*) *Fire ...*
Q Fire?
A (*Subject breaks into screams of uncontrollable terror and intensity which last for thirty seconds before she responds to the hypnotist's increasingly urgent command to return to the present*)

As she drifted up to the surface of consciousness she was told repeatedly that she would remember everything that she had seen, but would feel no pain of whatever had happened. When she was awake she was easily the most relaxed person in the room, and described how she had been lying on the floor of a building unable to move while flames licked round her body.

It is interesting that when subjects return to a waking state the memories of these new experiences are as clear and as real as those of important events in their present life. They can generally give a much fuller picture of what was happening than they could under hypnosis because they are now using their normal vocabulary, and are no longer limited by the strange restriction on language which is discussed later.

In a first regression the voice is almost always very quiet indeed, often inaudible, and understanding is further hindered by a slight slurring of the speech as in mild intoxication. There are long silences as the subject struggles with the strange situation, and questions have to be repeated again and again in different forms in the hope of striking a sympathetic chord. The answers are often brief, monosyllabic and obvious, and it seems as if the character is at best co-operating under compulsion, or at worst being deliberately obstructive and frustrating. This is illustrated in the opening session by the articulate American businessman Michael O'Mara, who as a Director of the publisher of this book felt that in the interests of integrity he must experience regression himself if possible. Several minutes of questioning brought no response, and then:

Q Have you any memories at all? Have you any memories? What can you remember?
A (*very very faintly*) Ah.
Q What can you remember?
A (*faintly, slurred*) Dunnow.
Q You *can* see something though, can't you? Come on, it does not matter how silly it seems, tell us. *What do you see?*
A Lossahats.
Q Lots of hats? Where are they?
A On heads.
Q On the heads of whom?
A People.
Q Yes, I know they are on the heads of people. What kinds of hats are they?
A Round hats.
Q Where are you standing? Or are you sitting, or what?
A Watching.
Q Watching what? Where from?
A The street.
Q What are you doing in the street?
A (*long pause*) Standing …

As the regression continues the speech tends to become clearer, louder and more continuous, though many subjects, even after a number of hours, will volunteer nothing beyond the bare minimum needed to answer the question they have been asked. From the very beginning too the observer is aware of the subject's problem with language, and his struggle to find the right

Carl Jung. Through his psychoanalytic investigations, Jung became increasingly interested in psychic experiences and developed the shadow-anima theory which Michael O'Mara illustrates so well

vocabulary. Some resort to simple and vague mime, not so much to convey their meaning to the others but more to remind themselves of the word they want with one half of their mind but cannot find with the other. Often they will have to make do with what is available: Sue Atkins, ironically enough for a professional lexicographer, found considerable difficulty in the early stages with the twelve-year-old urchin, Charlie.

Q Have you any beds in the room?
A We've got ... a ma ... m ... mat ... mat ... a mmmmmmmmmm ... a bag filled with straw.

Another frustrating characteristic is the refusal of some subjects to commit themselves to positive facts – not only dates and places, but also such basic information as their own names. They invent devious ways of avoiding definite statements, and sceptics seize on this as evidence of something suspicious: fact, they say, can be checked, and the regressee, perhaps involuntarily, senses a trap that will expose the whole thing as fantasy. Dorothy Hitchens, an office manager with a large insurance company, 'became' a young woman very unhappily married to a prosperous elderly farmer named Thomas in the seventeenth century, and after several sessions was moved forwards five years.

Q What happened to Tom then?
A Oh, thank God, he died.
Q (*sharply, trying to catch her off guard as she had steadily refused to give her husband's surname*) What *was* Tom's name? Tom what?
A (*pause – slight confusion*) Oh ... Tom ... Tom ... I forget about him – not worth bothering about.
Q By the way, I don't know *your* name.
A (*pause*) Oh ... oh ... Pat.
Q Pat what?
A (*pause*) Oh ... everybody calls me Pat.
Q You don't know your second name?
A I ... I ... don't use it.
Q But if I wanted to send you a letter, how should I address it?
A I ... I ... (*very confused and embarrassed*) I *really* don't know ...
Q But I would have to address it to someone, wouldn't I?
A (*changing tactics – very sharp and aggressive*) Of course you would ... Good Heavens ... (*another change of tactic – suddenly the pathetic whine of the frail little woman*) Oh ... Oh ... I keep having these upsets ...

Different subjects have different techniques for avoiding questions which objectively are innocent enough but which part of their mind finds threatening. A few adopt the obvious method of remaining silent, but most feel the need to use a more positive escape route. Edna Greenan as Nell Gwynn, for example, will either change the discussion abruptly, or else, if pinned down, will become drunk herself or else offer the questioner a glass of gin.

Q Now, Nell, who else was in the play?
A Ah...
Q You *must* know who was acting with you?
A Ah... (*pause*) ... Now something funny happened to Pippy [Pepys] the other day ...

Observers who expect exotic personalities talking in incomprehensible languages to emerge at Keeton's sessions are likely to be disappointed as only a very small number indeed belong to anything but the last three centuries. The spontaneous outpourings in fluent Sanskrit or Aramaic that one reads about just do not seem to exist: there is, as we have seen, a marked narrowing of language skills, and subjects who have a long-standing proficiency in a foreign language are generally quite incapable of using it or even recognizing it if the personality to whom they have regressed could not have done so. An honours graduate in French and German had regressed to a lad in Bristol in the fifteenth century, and described how he often went on the quays to talk to the seamen who had come from foreign ports:

Q You say you can understand French, so if someone spoke to you in French you would know what they were saying?
A They say things like "Bee ... enn'
Q What does that mean?
A It means 'Come here'.
Q [Asked by a Frenchwoman who feels very deeply about the correctness of accent and grammar] Avez-vous déja monté sur le bateau?
A (*puzzled silence for some seconds, then tentatively*) Bateau?
Q What does that mean?
A Bateau is a boat.
Q Vous êtes allé en France sur un bateau?
A (*very long pause*) That's how they speak ... *something* like that.

In perhaps ninety-nine per cent of the cases, subjects use modern language patterns and pronunciation for almost any identity even though the English speech of only a century ago would have been very different from today's, and that of the fifteenth century virtually incomprehensible. There appears to be an occasional compulsion to use stereotyped archaisms such as 'Aye', 'Nay', 'Sire' and 'prithee', but these seem almost as if the conscious mind is trying to add a period flavour rather like a Hollywood film, to save its own face.

The problem of the language a subject uses worries some observers who feel that for a regression to be genuine, the personality should speak exactly as it would at the time at which it claimed to have lived. But it may be that even if the unconscious is thinking in another language, the motor mechanisms of speech are still under the control of the conscious which acts instinctively as a machine translating the thoughts into current vocabulary and constructions. The 'Petros' sequence on page 23 seems to show that the inner part of the mind can read in one language, while the other part speaks the words in a different tongue, but actually listens to them in the first.

All of these things the outsider can observe for himself, but he can, of course, see only the exterior manifestations of what is going on inside the subject's mind. What is happening behind those closed eyes is, as in all other aspects of hypnosis, intensely personal and very variable, but certain patterns do seem to be common to a large number of those who can analyse afterwards what they actually saw and felt at the time.

As Keeton's voice tells them that the clocks are running backwards and that they are free to search for a memory in all time, the conscious mind feels that chill panic that strikes most people when, on their first flight, the wheels leave the familiar and secure solidity of earth for the unknown and un-natural realm of the air. At first there is usually nothing but impenetrable blackness in which the conscious mind, struggling for control, fights to form an image. Nothing emerges, but the voice beats on: Where are you? What do you see? You have complete memories – what IS happening?

Then, sometimes gradually, sometimes suddenly, the darkness begins to solidify: a face, an object or part of a scene resolves itself mistily, uncertainly, and for most subjects it is at first motionless, monochrome and softened like a faded Victorian photograph. The new eye seems to concentrate on one small part of the whole, clinging desperately to keep it in being and in focus, lest it vanish.

Light Profile by Odilon Redon. Many subjects speak about the sensation of standing outside themselves

This first image can be something quite consciously remembered from the old world of reality and installed in the new – perhaps the waking mind is still struggling to hold on to its vanishing empire. The opening of one of the American regressions is typical of this attempt to bridge the divisions of the mind. Thelma Palmer was asked as soon as she had shown the signs of being alive in her new personality:

Q What do you see?
A A door.
Q What colour is this door?
A Afraid to go in.
Q Are you inside or outside the door?
A Outside.
Q Where does the door lead?
A To the kitchen.

Although she knew quite well at that moment the new personality was in Pennsylvania in the late-eighteenth century, the door she saw so clearly was the one belonging to the cottage where she stayed in England, correct in every detail down to the last iron stud.

Often, even though the image can be seen so clearly, no voice can be found to describe it. The conscious mind could do so easily, but its links with the speech mechanisms seem to be broken, and the effect is that of the picture babbling soundlessly from the TV when a cable in the studio has become accidentally disconnected. Keeton's relentless, questioning voice flows on, cajoling, urging, commanding: You *do* have complete memories … You *can* see what is happening … You *must* tell us what you see … Where are you?

As the last faint grip of the conscious slips away, even if temporarily, the picture clears, takes on muted shades which harden into natural colours, and movement begins, sometimes quite normally, sometimes jerkily at the beginning like a slow-run film or a succession of stills. A voice, as we have seen, hesitant, confused, slurred and restricted begins to answer dreamily. The waking mind surrenders finally to become only a critical, rationalizing but completely passive and helpless observer of what the other part is doing and saying – but all the time it is poised to intervene and to reassert its authority if an opportunity should arise.

Gradually details begin to flow more freely, but while the description of the woods or streets, people or traffic may be fairly complete the personality at the centre of it, observing and reporting, often remains a complete enigma to itself. It does not know its name, the period in which it is living, whether it is male or female, or how old it is. Even if it is aware that it is doing something very positive, such as running furiously or fighting, it has usually no idea at first why it is doing so. If a subject does find himself at the opening in one of these desperate situations, he often becomes very angry in his helpless conscious mind because as well as struggling to establish an identity he has not only to fight off an enemy, swim a flooded river or mount the gallows, but also to endure idiot voices battering him with such inanities as 'How old are you?', 'What colour is your hair?', 'Are you a little boy or a little girl?'

How subjects perceive all of this material varies: some stay throughout their regressions outside their 'body' looking as it were at the events unfolding on some private cinema screen. They know precisely which character they are in the picture, and though they are quite detached from the action, they feel all the pains, pleasures and emotions. Other subjects experience the whole episode as if they were actually inside the body of the new personality, feeling everything through his sense organs, though of course the sight must be inward rather than outward.

The information a subject produces in answer to questions seems to appear in the mind sometimes as a concept, sometimes as pictures. Some people say that the reply flashes in as an abstract thought which immediately transforms itself into an image, while others have a visual impression first which then becomes thought or speech. But in both cases the time between thinking and seeing, or seeing and thinking is so brief that it is often difficult to decide which really began the sequence.

In most situations the imagery is quite normal: a general question such as 'What can you see?' will quite logically produce details of the room, the street or the landscape which the personality is viewing at that moment, but occasionally a more specific request will irrationally evoke a written answer in the subject's mind. The urchin Charlie (Sue Atkins), for example, was asked the name of the village where he lived – a question which had been put to him several times previously but which he had been unable to answer. At each 'Don't know' he had become increasingly distressed but this time, in the middle of a sequence in which he had been describing what was happening in the small village school, he replied after only a brief hesitation 'Willingford'. Sue said when she was wakened that Charlie had felt the usual panic, but almost at once saw the word written in childish hand superimposed on the scene at which he was looking.

Wherever the material comes from, and however it is presented, the conscious watches, listens, reasons and often experiences its own emotions, very different from those of the unconscious acting through the new character. The waking mind will often jeer at the way the subject's regressed personality claims to be able to look forward and backwards at the same time, to see the inside and outside of a building simultaneously and to know what is inside a locked door it has never entered. It is furious when its other self makes what it considers stupid mistakes. Thelma Palmer as Tom Brown in Philadelphia in about 1784 was asked:

Q Have you a dollar? (*puzzled silence*) What is a dollar, Tom?
A A dollar? A dollar?
Q What is the smallest coin you have?
A (*exasperated as if talking to an idiot*) A penny, of course.

Q And the largest?
A A shilling.

When Thelma was wakened she said that her conscious mind was disgusted
that as Tom Brown she was making herself seem such a fool: everyone in
the room knew that Tom was in post-revolutionary America, and here he
was babbling like an idiot of British shillings and pence. When the point
was checked it was found that the dollar did not become the official unit of
currency for the US until 1786, and even long after this, the old British
system of pounds, shillings and pence, continued to be used just as they did
when Britain herself adopted a decimal coinage in 1971.

Sometimes, but very rarely, the conscious is highly amused by the antics
and attitudes of the personality it cannot control – perhaps it finds poking
fun one way of getting a little revenge. Sue Atkins as the pious, humourless
priest Father Antony Bennet in the second half of the seventeenth century
was being asked about the political situation in England after the
Restoration.

Q Who runs the government?
A The government ... is the king. Charles the Second ... the devil king.
Q Why the devil king?
A (*extremely pompously*) Charles whores ... Charles makes promises ...
Charles uses promises as other men use tools ...

Someone in the room whispered to another 'If Charles whores I should say
that promises are not the only tool he uses ...' and quietly though it was
said, both Father Bennet and Sue Atkins heard. The unconscious mind set
the face of the priest into a stony scowl of disapproval – or perhaps incom-
prehension – while the conscious shook with invisible and unheard
laughter.

Perhaps the emotion that the conscious experiences most frequently is
amazement as it listens to the voice which it has for so long dominated now
acting quite independently and producing completely unknown material.
The facts seem to well up from nowhere and the first knowledge the waking
mind has of them is when it hears them spoken aloud. Examples occur in
almost every regression, and range from trivial domestic details to wider
and more public issues.

However helpless the conscious may seem to itself and to the observers it
never gives up the struggle of trying to reassert its lost influence over the
thought processes. It does not take over completely of course, as that would
mean the end of the regression, but it does come much nearer to the surface.
Sometimes when a subject is tired and cannot find the answer to a question,
the unconscious seems to back away to allow that other part of the mind at
least to suggest an answer. This is not generally a directly recalled piece of
information, but it certainly does not come from the deepest levels, and falls
on the listening ear with a definite familiarity. Over and over again it is

found in regression that when some element of the waking mind seems to be prompting the unconscious the answer is incorrect: the conscious half-remembers, reasons, rationalizes – and comes up with something which seems to have some relevance, but has more of the schoolboy howler. If the deeper layers of the mind are given their head, they may produce a great deal of unimportant, irrelevant and uncheckable matter but buried among this are those astounding facts that make the whole of regression such a fascinating study.

Anything up to four hours after those first words 'Search out a memory …' there comes the return to the world of the present. In a few cases where a very distressing experience occurs a subject is brought out instantly, perhaps after only five or ten minutes: in a good many an hour has exhausted all that is obviously going to be obtained, but in a small number exciting incident after exciting incident pours out until it is only exhaustion – on the part of the questioners, not the subject – that compels Joe Keeton to go into the waking routine.

If it is a fairly routine regression there is a short break for drinks and then a new subject sits in the chair to attempt the long journey back. But if it is an exciting new personality or one that is being studied more carefully there will be considerable discussion as the subject now awake can add a great deal of detail about the personality, its appearance, surrounding, memories and emotions. When asked why they did not give these under hypnosis the reply is inevitably that they were not asked: Ann Dowling as the orphan Sarah has been regressed so many times that she is very aware how important this additional material is, but says that although the conscious is anxious to tell the group, the unconscious forbids it unless the facts have been specifically requested.

3. Real Reincarnation?

Ann Dowling

Some subjects seem only to make the problem of offering an answer to regression more confusing: there is no doubt that something remarkable is happening, but the arguments for and against each of the possible explanations seem almost to cancel each other out. Yet at the end a massive amount of material remains which no one can dismiss as fraud, imagination or fantasy, and one feels that either some factor has been overlooked or else a completely unconsidered principle is operating. Other regressions point much more specifically towards a single explanation, and one wonders why anything else was considered – until another subject produces material which apparently indicates with equal certainty a completely different solution.

If one were looking for a case history that suggested quite simply that some form of reincarnation was the only answer one could not do better than listen to forty-seven-year-old Ann Dowling, a working-class housewife from Huyton who in more than sixty hours of regression has consistently become Sarah Williams, an orphan living in the slums of Everton in the first half of the nineteenth century. Not only does Sarah produce a steady stream of very obscure facts that no one could possibly know without months of research, but also she gives a brilliantly illuminating picture of how life and the world must have seemed to a naive, credulous and illiterate girl of the streets whose only source of information was half-heard and quarter-understood gossip which was probably only a travesty of the truth in the first place. Through Sarah we can really feel the bigotry, the folk-feeling of the gutter, and the animal-like acceptance of unbelievable conditions of hunger, cold and misery of the very poorest level of industrial revolution society. How can Ann, unless some part of her present being already experienced it, produce such material as the following extracts? She has no idea of course until she is actually under hypnosis to which period she is being sent: on this occasion it was 1850.

Q What's happening in Liverpool, Sarah?
A Ah ... there's a lady bin ... she sings ...
Q Oh, what is her name?
A Ah ... summat to do wi' a bird ... a bird ... a little bird ...
Q Robin? Sparrow?
A It's a bird ... she's foreign ...

On 8 August 1850 Jenny Lind, the Swedish Nightingale, arrived in Liverpool from Stockholm to sail to Boston, and sang for two nights at the Philharmonic Hall.

How could anyone, unless they had once actually believed it, produce such a bizarre conception of Heaven and Hell as Sarah did at the age of twenty.

Q How do you get to heaven, Sarah?
A When you're dead ... this is what The Thumper ses – well, you go an' see God an' if you've bin a little bit bad ... you go to a place where it's nice and warm.
Q But not too hot?
A (*completely ignoring the question*) An' if you've bin a bit more bad, well, you go to 'Ell ... an' nobody never goes to 'Eaven ... Well ... you go an' be good so as you can see God ... and 'E'll send you to 'Ell.
Q That seems a bit complicated, Sarah. What is this Heaven where your dad is?
A Oh ... it's nice there ... but I 'aven't bin ... But you can look down ... out of the sky ... an' see all the people you want to see.
Q Do they do anything else in Heaven?
A Yuh ... you get wings ... an' stick 'em on their back.
Q And why do they do that?
A (*pause ... puzzled*) I ... think it is so they can go for ... no ... well ... Thumper said you could go from one cloud to another. (*pause ... very worried by something that has obviously struck her*) But you can't do that ... 'cos some days there isn't any ...

Jenny Lind. She visited Liverpool in 1850 to sing at the Philharmonic Hall

Q When you have these wings, what happens then?
A You're an' angel then ... an' they gorra golden thing round their 'ead as
   well.
Q Is it hair?
A (*scandalized*) *No* ... it's goodness ...

Ann originally approached Joe Keeton because of two recurrent nightmares
which for many years had followed invariably the same sequence: in one she
was sitting alone in a small bare room, completely bewildered and with a
growing sense of terrible apprehension, and in the other she was standing in
a sordid basement with a roughly dressed stranger brandishing a knife. In
her dreams she never found out why she was so filled with dread in the first,
nor what happened in the second, but both always left her very disturbed
for much of the following day.
    In her first regression the stark reality of both situations became horrify-
ingly clear as memory pulled back the curtains to reveal the whole scene
instead of the tiny detail seen through the gap of dreaming.

Q You have a complete set of memories ... you are free in all time ... you can remember everything ... where are you? Where are you?

A (*instantly a terrified panting*) In ... a ... basement.

Q What kind of room?

A (*voice tight with terror*) In ... a ... basement.

Q What is your name?

A (*frightened whisper*) Aha ... aha ... Sarah ... aha ... I ... ca ... ca ... (*hysterically*) I ... don't ... like ... this ... room.

Q I know you don't. But we want to help you. Give us a description of the room. Where is this room?

A In a house.

Q I know it is in a house, but in which town? Where *IS* this house?

A Oh ... ah ... it ... ah ... it ... Chaucer Road.

Q Chaucer Road? But where? Which town?

A Don't know (*shouts in panic*) Don't like ... this room. Don't like ... this ... room.

Q Who is with you?

A Lindy ... and Tony ... and Jimmy an' Jacky ...

Q If all of these people are with you, why are you so afraid?

A I ... don't ... like ... this ... room ...

Sarah was told to go into a deep sleep and brought forward five years: her head dropped forward, her breathing became deep and regular, but she would not respond to any questions – the usual sign that the personality was dead. Keeton told her to return to the previous period, and instantly the frantic heaving of the chest began and the face contorted with terror.

Q Where are you now?

A (*breathless with fear*) In ... that ... room ... I don't like ... this ... room.

Q I know you don't, Sarah, but why are you so frightened? Why don't you like this room?

A It's that man ... it's ... that man.

Q What man? *Remember.*

A AAAh ... ahhh ... (*breaks down in bitter crying*) Get ... the kids out.

Q All right, Sarah. We'll get the kids out.

A Oh ... he's ... got ... got ... got a big ... it's like ... a ... knife. (*screaming*) He's hitting me ... He's coming ... *coming* ...

Before she went silent with a sharp cry of anguish, she gasped out at Keeton's repeated demand, a vague description of a rough man whom she thought was an Irish navvy from the railway building whom she had seen on a previous occasion lurking in an alley as she took the four children she was minding back to their parents.

On the theory that subjects under regression strike first the most traumatic experience of their existences, this was not a particularly unusual episode among the thousands that Joe Keeton had listened to over the years, but the way in which it amplified and illuminated Ann's nightmare seemed to be very significant. In an attempt to see if there was another story which would throw a similar light on the other recurrent dream, Sarah was taken back to her early childhood.

Initially there emerged an interesting but in no way extraordinary picture of a five-year-old girl, Sarah Williams, in the 1830s living alone with her father – her mother having died in childbirth – in a tiny house in the maze of terraced rows near the bustling harbour of a large city. Sarah's father, Joseph, was a casual dock labourer and though the wages of a man fortunate to have regular full-time work were pitiful enough, it seems that he often worked only half a day in order to spend more time with his child. By purely material standards life in the little house was hard and rough, the immensely warm bond between father and daughter compensated for any deficiencies in food, clothing and comfort. 'When me dad has a ship, he buys potatoes,' Sarah's favourite food: sometimes ''e jus' puts them on the fire ... an' it makes 'em nice': 'me dad's a lot bigger'n me ... he has to bend down to give me a lift.' 'Me dad' calls her 'his little gipsy' and somehow acquires a doll and a hoop from a barrel on the docks for her to play with. On one very special occasion he brought her home a pair of shoes – in a much later regression she said that these were the only ones she ever had.

Moving and pathetic though some of the anecdotes were they were not unique: after all, millions of people could produce similar stories from their present lives, but it was felt that somewhere among the rather vague memories of 'me dad' there lay the key to the second nightmare. Sarah was brought forward one month and immediately she began wringing her hands and her whole demeanour conveyed a sense of deep distress. Her father had not come home from work. She indignantly dismissed suggestions that he might have gone for a drink;

A 'e don' drink ... it's bad. Me dad *will* come ... 'E wouldn't leave me on me own ...
Q What will you do if he doesn't come home?
A (*confidence beginning to ooze away*) 'E ... 'e'll ... come ... 'ome.
Q You are not going to look for him?
A (*now thoroughly afraid*) No ... 'e wouldn't like ... me to go away.

Sarah was now becoming very distressed indeed, twisting her hands together and sobbing bitterly. She was told to come forward half an hour, but her grief was so obvious that every question had initially to be repeated several times.

Q What *is* the matter, Sarah?
A (*breaks down completely*) 'E ... 'e ... 'e ... 'e said ... my dad ... isn't ... comin' ... 'ome.
Q Who said that?
A (*still sobbing desperately*) That ... man ... 'E said ... 'is name was Johnson.

Q What exactly did he tell you, Sarah?
A (*long sobbing pause*) 'E ... said ... 'e said ... a horse done something ... to me dad ...'N' 'e said ... me dad ... wasn't comin' 'ome ... An' I'll have to go away with 'im ... to a 'ome ... 'n' *I wasn't bad* ... I wasn't bad. 'E said ... a 'orse done something ... terrible ... to 'im.
Q Don't you think you should go to Mrs Vaughan (*a neighbour*)?
A Noo ... I'll wait until ... me dad ... comes ... 'ome ... 'E will ... come ... 'ome ... 'e wouldn't leave me (*breaks down completely*) I ... want ... me ... dad.

The significance of Ann's second nightmare was becoming apparent, though the full meaning did not become clear until some time later when Sarah was taken to an hour after the visit by her father's employer, Mr Johnson. It is perhaps with the following episode that the immense importance of Ann's regression began to make itself apparent as she recalled – or recreated – what must have happened so many times in the squalor, the poverty and the desperation of the poorest levels in society, when any scruples were sub-servient to the sheer necessity of surviving. Morality, like food, clothing and warmth, was a luxury that could rarely be afforded in the stinking courts, alleys and tenements of the labouring classes in the bursting new cities of the industrial revolution. Sarah was no longer sobbing, but seemed stunned. She said she was sitting in the kitchen ... waiting.

Q Has anyone been to see you?
A (*dead flat*) Mrs Vaughan.
Q And what did she say?
A She said ... I was bad ... an' me dad (*sob*) worked (*sob*) too hard for me (*sob*) I'm not ... bad.
Q What did Mrs Vaughan do then?
A (*violently between sobs*) She ... borrowed ... the ... chairs.
Q What all of them?
A We've only got two.
Q What did she say she was borrowing them for?
A She ... kept ... saying I was ... bad. (*weeps*) I'm not ... bad ... 'N' she said he worked ... too 'ard for ... me. (*long pause*) When me dad comes back ... 'e'll get 'em back ... 'e will.

To see the outcome of this sordid sequence Sarah was brought forward another five hours: she was still in the kitchen, still alone, still unfed. She was now utterly dejected and broken, and convinced her father was not coming home.

Q Has anybody been to see you?
A Mrs Farmer.
Q And what did she come for?
A They took the mugs ... and the table.

Q Didn't you say you didn't want them to take them?
A I told them me dad'd shout.
Q And what did they say?
A (*very puzzled*) They said 'e'd 'ave a job.
Q What else did they take?
A There's on'y the bed left now.
Q Have you any blankets?
A No.

In a later regression Sarah was taken back again to this incident and described in more details how the moment the news of her father's death reached the neighbours they swarmed round the little house like vultures, eager to snatch up any of the pathetic possessions that still remained. In a dead, stunned voice she says 'Cissie from next door upstairs 's took the bed …' and repeats Mrs Vaughan's callous comment 'You won't need nothing where you're goin''. The only person who showed any humanity at this period was Mr Johnson, but perhaps in his prosperity he could afford to. He told Sarah the day after her father's death that he would keep an eye on her and that 'it' was all for her own good, but the bewildered six-year-old could not comprehend what 'it' might mean. It was only when Mr Johnson came accompanied by a black horse with a 'funny carriage' on which was a box containing, he said, Sarah's father, that realization dawned that life as she had known it was at an end. There was a very distressing scene:

A That's … not … me … dad. (*bursts into tears*) *That's … not … me … dad … in … that … box …* It's not … me dad.
Q Who says it is your dad?
A (*crying bitterly*) 'E says … that's … me … dad … that … Mr Johnson. They're goin' away … takin' the box … (*screaming*) *That's … not … me … dad.*

Mr Johnson told the little girl he would call the following day to take her to a home, and probably quite sincerely did not realize the child had not eaten for three days: but during that night Sarah grew immeasurably older, and made the great decision of her life, however wrong it might have been. Between these two cardinal points in her life – the death of her father when she was six and her own death twenty or so years later – there unfolds a remarkably convincing regression. Little of importance on the larger scale occurs, but it is just because it is such a non-existence, packed with minute personal details, that it is so credible.

Sarah's life falls into two distinct periods. In the first, rather than go into a 'home' ('only bad people go into th'ome … You go from th'ome to th'ospital, and from th'ospital to th' graveyard') she runs away and for the next ten years lives like a stray dog, finding shelter in alleys, in doorways, and on luckier nights in the nightwatchman's hut. For part of this period she was befriended by a Mr and Mrs Roper who often allowed her to sleep on the floor of their lobby where, even if it was cold and hard, it was at least dry and reasonably free from draughts. The Ropers, who had four daughters of their own, handed on clothing from time to time though they were only working people themselves, and shielded the little waif from the worst pangs of hunger. For the rest, she scrubbed steps at a farthing a time – among the working classes the gleaming white front doorstep was almost an obsession, and probably the only concession to respectability they could afford.

As Ann began to get deeper and deeper into the regression the little domestic details that characterize Sarah began to emerge, and it is these, which surprised the subject as much as the observers, that make the whole series so credible and fascinating.

Sarah commented that sometimes people gave her a 'wedge' when she did the steps: under hypnosis she could explain no more than that it was a 'wedge' but awake she said that it was a hunk of bread. When asked where she kept her money because she had said that she had nothing but a dress on, Ann twisted the bottom of her skirt in both hands and said, 'I ties it in me 'em' – and again, when awake she was astounded as she had never remotely visualized such a trick. The second period of Sarah's life began when she was about fifteen and was forced to find a permanent sleeping place under cover because, she said, the police would take her up if she stayed out at night for being 'a certain kind of woman' – though it is difficult to imagine how the most prudish constable could have imagined the filthy, ragged, shoeless and disfigured girl was a prostitute.

As Mrs Roper was now dead she eventually found squalid accommodation in the basement of a person she refers to as Eric Wiseman (Weitzmann or some variation) who, she said, either owned, or was agent for, a number of slum houses. Sarah describes with disgust how Wiseman collected the rents and how if the occupants could not pay threw them into the street, confiscating their pitiful belongings in lieu. These, which consisted mainly of ragged clothing, he stored in the cellar where Sarah found shelter, and here, amid the stinking, verminous garments, the rats, and without a single stick of furniture, she passed the rest of her life – and indeed, here she died.

In return for this security Sarah had to clean Wiseman's house, but as he paid her nothing and did not even allow her any food, she was thrown more than ever on the charity she so much hated. In almost every regression she repeated one of her father's basic principles: 'Me dad ses it's all charity ... an' you don't 'ave charity from nobody. If you don't earn it then you don't 'ave it ... that's what me dad ses, and it's right.' Sarah had said that Wiseman lived in Shaw Street, and later when asked the number mimed '5 ... 7'. Gore's Directory for Liverpool for 1843 gives the resident of 57 Shaw Street as Emmanuel Zwilchenbart, a merchant and also Swiss consul. There may be an intriguing mystery here: 'Wiseman' is Jewish and there are long sequences later when Sarah describes the Sabbath and other rituals. Somehow, too, she confuses him with his friend 'Polish' who 'doesn't speak like us', which probably indicates that 'Polish' is a nationality rather than a name. It would be interesting to know if Emmanuel Zwilchenbart was Jewish – he might well be the original Wiseman whose name has been vaguely remembered and anglicized.

Sarah at fifteen was too old to scrub steps and had it not been for Mrs Roper's daughter Teresa, who had married a rather well-to-do man and who felt under an obligation to carry on her mother's kindness to the orphan, she would have been in dire straits. Although Teresa's husband, an American called James Wannamaker, disliked the girl – Sarah says this because of the terrible purple birthmark on her face – she was still given cast-off clothes and occasional meals. In return, and perhaps to allay her deep-seated fear and hatred of charity, Sarah looked after the Wannamaker children, and it was these whom she begged to be taken from the room in the murder sequence.

In the twenty years of drab, and by our standards utterly miserable existence covered by Sarah's regressions, there are a number of closely-interwoven elements. First, and most important from a technical point of view, are the precise details of her everyday life – eating, sleeping, working, shopping, washing, hygiene, clothing, gossip, and menstruating – and the way these are linked to local events, topography and personalities that are checkable, even if with difficulty. It is the very unimportance of these events that are so important: there seems no way in which Ann Dowling could find out this trivial, but immensely telling, detail. As she is never told in advance to which period of her life she is being taken, five, fifteen or twenty-five, there is no way in which she can prepare even a skeleton of facts beforehand, and yet the flow of anecdote, comment and description begins instantly. If only we could place complete historical trust in the accuracy of some of this unknown material that Sarah produces it would give us a completely new insight into the social life of a sub-culture that is so inadequately documented just because it was regarded at the time as being largely sub-human.

The second element is the completely convincing re-creation of the life of the poor of the period and the way they accept their lot of cold, hunger and discomfort not as deprivation and injustice, but as the normal structure of society: here we see Disraeli's famous 'two worlds' of later in the century become a living reality and not just a political catchphrase. The way in which Sarah acknowledges without a trace of self-pity or envy the gulf between herself and 'the posh people up the hill' makes the Victorians a little more understandable.

Thirdly, although Ann herself is half-Irish, is happily married to an Irishman, and was brought up a Catholic, the whole of her regression is a savage tirade against the Irish and Roman Catholics in general. Sarah reflects in miniature all the bigoted, bitter and ignorant sectarian hatred that has tortured Ireland for centuries – but ironically, from a strictly Protestant point of view.

Lastly, although the personality of Sarah is entirely without a glimmer of humour, the regressions are often riotous. Her gutter gossip, her literal interpretation of words as she hears them, her misunderstandings and her *naïveté* frequently reduce everyone present to helpless laughter – and all the while Sarah sits primly, pursing her lips, half-puzzled, half-petulant that some innocent and deadly serious remark she has made has caused such amusement. Herself, the only amusing thing she remembers is when The Thumper, a hell-fire-and-damnation itinerant preacher she mentions frequently, fell over.

Sarah's territory is the central part of Liverpool mainly in the vicinity of Byrom Street – a street with which Ann Dowling is completely unfamiliar though she does know the more famous roads. Her home with her father, she says, was in Chaucer Street, which is in the right area, and although today it is largely modern flats, it was an area of poor housing early in the nineteenth century.

On one occasion she was being asked about illness, but said that she was never ill – she only had pains: 'Growing pains – you gotta have pains so as yer bones can grow'.

Q Is there a chemist's shop where you are? Do you know what a chemist is?
A Ah – shop where you get medicine?
Q That's right. Have you ever been in that shop?
A *Oh no.* Don't know what they'd give yuh. I seen in the window once ... didn't like the bottles. (*she went on to describe the traditional three-coloured jars*)
Q Do you know the name of the shop?
A (*pause*) Ah ... Sampsons ... its got a funny word what nobody can say ... I wish I could read ...

The early street directories show that John and James Sampson, chemists and druggists, had a shop at 50 Byrom Street in 1839, and then at 103 Byrom Street until 1848, when they disappear from the scene. It seems almost impossible that Ann Dowling could possibly have unearthed the name of this long-vanished business, but it is typical of the obscure flashes that keep turning up throughout her regression. Many months later Sarah spoke suddenly of fires.

A There's one place an' it burnt down twice but that's a long time ago.
Q And what was that called?
A Aw ... it's ... um ... I don't know the word ... but you know that shop that's got all them coloured bottles in ...
Q I don't know it but you have talked about it.
A Well, it belongs to them ... where you get medicine ... the big building had these little shops what sold medicine ... it burnt down twice.

Can this possibly explain Sampson's move from no. 50 to no. 103, and then their disappearance from Byrom Street altogether?

When conversation with Sarah seemed to be lagging the question 'What's been happening in Liverpool?' or 'Has anyone important been to Liverpool?' often brings a startling answer, as in the following widely separated sequences.

Q Has anyone been to visit Liverpool – important people?
A Well (*long pause*) 'e's sposed to be a prince ... but 'is dad's *not* a king.
Q Oh? How can he be a prince if his dad is not a king?
A 'E's one of them foreign ones.
Q Oh – what was his name?
A Ah ... No ... I think 'e was from ... *Russia* ... They 'ave a lotta that now.
Q Lot of what Sarah?
A Lotta them foreign ones come 'ere ... 'cos the Queen ... 's's foreign.

The final phrase probably referred to Albert because Sarah had mentioned him several times and was rather worried that he was foreign. While with many subjects this rather odd reference to a 'prince ... but 'is dad's not a king' might have been passed over as an irrelevance, Sarah's previous record made it worthwhile checking. The date to which she had been taken was somewhere in the mid-1840s, and amazingly an obscure newspaper item for 14 March 1846 reported that Prince d'Musignana, son of Lucien Buonaparte and nephew of Emperor Napoleon, had arrived in Liverpool on the steamer *Cambria* on his way from Boston to France and Italy.

Royal visits, as always, made a great impression and the excitement obviously filtered down through the levels of society from the fashionable streets about the city centre to the courts and alleys of the slums. Sarah mentions the Queen and Prince Albert on many occasions, but two are particularly significant. Both occurred in the same session, and though the period is rather vague, they can be dated between 1846 and 1852.

Q Are there any famous people living in Shaw Street?
A I don' know if there is now.
Q Who used to be there? Anybody famous you used to know?
A Oh ... I didn't know them.
Q But you know the name, don't you?
A Well ... you've heard ... you know when Victoria's husband ... *Albert* ... when's 'e came ... 'e stayed there.
Q Did he?
A With a judge.

Albert did visit Liverpool on his own in July 1846 and stayed at the lodgings of Judge William Wharton, not actually in Shaw Street, but in St Anne Street not far away. It is interesting to note that Sarah referred to the incident above as in the past, but the following episode, which followed about a quarter of an hour later, she indicates is very recent.

Q Anything been happening in Liverpool? Any visitors? Any big fires?
A The Queen's bin.

Q Did she come on her own?

A (*scandalized*) *Oh no* … she's married now … she can't go out on her own. No.

Q Where did they stay? Did the Queen stay in Shaw Street?

A On a boat.

Q What was the name of the boat?

A (*silence, but childish giggles from Sarah*)

Q What are you laughing at?

A Well … it makes me think of something … well … what I heard when I was little.

Q Go on.

A Well … it's called *The Fairy* … a fairy is … little tiny things what fly around … but they're nice.

Everyone in the room knew that the royal yacht was the *Victoria and Albert*, and again the strange name Fairy was an aberration, but it was checked in the newspaper archives. The *Victoria and Albert* anchored in the harbour, but all of the tours of inspection were made in the royal tender, which was called *The Fairy*.

Sarah is constantly mentioning big fires, but as the records show almost annual outbursts in which warehouses and sometimes whole streets are gutted no real significance can be attached to them. There are two rather extraordinary references to lighting however. At a date which seemed to be

Prince Albert visited Liverpool in 1846, touring the docks in the tender which Ann correctly named *The Fairy*

in the 1840s Sarah was talking about 'Old Wiseman' and his argument with 'Polish'.

A Mrs Roper kicked him down the steps once, y'know.
Q Why did she do that?
A He was being horrible.
Q In what way?
A He was going to stop people gettin' gas in their houses.
Q What did he want to do that for? (*silence*) What is this gas?
A (*excited*) You put a light to it an' it makes a light ... an' you don' have to have a candle.
Q Where does it come from?
A (*long puzzled pause*) The cocky watchman's 'ole, I think.

Gas lighting was extended to the suburbs and the poorer parts of Liverpool in the late 1830s and as always there was opposition, sometimes based on genuine fear, and sometimes on expense. Particularly as a small child in the 1830s Sarah mentions seeking refuge at night in the cocky's hut ('cocky' is a local idiom for a watchman) but apart from saying that he was watching a hole in the street she could say no more why he was there. It seems obvious that he was keeping guard over the trenches being dug for the gas mains. An even more off-beat reference came in a late regression when Sarah had been taken to the age of twenty-four, that is, the early 1850s.

A I heard somebody talking about somethin' an' it can't be real.
Q Why – what is it?
A Well – they're goin' to bring it to Liverpool to show the people.
Q But what is it?
A It's a new kind of light. It's a big word and you don' have to put a light to it.
Q It lights itself does it? What do they call it? Can you remember the word?
A (*long pause*) No ... it's big.
Q Where did you hear about it?
A I heard ... some people talkin' about it but ... they said ... it can't be true ... an' The Thumper said it's the work of the devil ... but they're goin' to bring it to Liverpool to show people ...

Although a dynamo capable of producing electricity on a commercial scale and also the incandescent bulb were well in the future and this demonstration must have been only a scientific novelty, there certainly was an exhibition of electric light on the landing stage on 7 July 1852.

One of the most intriguing aspects of Sarah's memories of people, places and events is the way so many of them are arbitrary, abstruse and as far as one can see, without any connection with her life. Why should a little gutter waif remember a brief flash of Jenny Lind and names of the royal tender and one chemist's shop while so much that was intimately connected with her life has vanished? But perhaps the most bizarre episode of all was when Sarah was asked what had been happening in Liverpool. She replied: 'They've taken our time away, they've stolen some of our minutes.' This seemed absolutely incomprehensible to everyone present. There did however seem a very faint echo of the mobs in 1752 howling 'They've taken twelve days off our lives' when Britain adopted the Gregorian calendar because the date and the sun's position had got out of step and 2 September that year was followed by 14 September. A report on Waterloo Observatory 1849–57 produces a very obscure and academic paper on synchronizing the times at the observatories of Greenwich and Liverpool – a difficult operation before radio or even a telegraph line. It was found that the port of Liverpool was 48.2 seconds behind Greenwich Mean Time, which though of little importance to most people, might have had some marginal effect on the navigation of ships across the Atlantic. Is it possible that the report of this stark little scientific exercise was passed on to lower and lower levels, distorted, twisted, misunderstood until when it reached the simple minds of Sarah's circle it loomed as a terrible threat?

When these strange incidents, however unlikely, seem to be substantiated by documentary evidence we must pay very serious attention to what Sarah says about material which there is little hope of checking. And even here, among a mass of personal detail which could be all fantasy or imagination there crop up from time to time these incredible, accurate, historical facts, as in this rather humdrum episode. Sarah has been taken to the age of ten.

Q Where do you eat?
A Sometimes when you scrub steps they give you a big wedge ... sometimes you get *cocoa* (*cocoa, together with potatoes, are the ultimate of Sarah's gastronomic horizons*)
Q Do you steal?
A Oh no *oh no* ... not with 'im coming round the corner.
Q Who is coming round the corner?
A The fat bobby ... Bobby Edwards.
Q You know him?
A He knows us all ... 'e's alright. Sometimes 'e gives us cocoa.

'Bobby' Edwards from Rosehill Police Station crops up constantly throughout the earlier period of Sarah's life as a step girl. He finds her shelter from time to time, gives her cocoa and advice, and acts generally as a protector as far as he can. Occasionally, according to Sarah, he is with P.C. Brownlow who is less sympathetic towards the homeless urchins, but fair and just. 'Bobby' Edwards looks like an archetype and certainly the police records for Liverpool have no record of a Constable Edwards or Brownlow at the period. Then, completely unexpectedly, a researcher found that in the 1840s Rosehill Police Station had an Inspector John Edwards who lived at Brownlow Terrace, Brownlow Street: one can except a few coincidences, but there does come a point when one must look for some other explanation.

The question of sheer survival – clothing, food or warmth – seemed so difficult that the observers came back to it again and again. Sarah as a step girl seemed to make no change, summer or winter: usually when asked, she was wearing only a dress, sometimes with a petticoat, and appeared genuinely puzzled when asked if she wore anything underneath. She had no shoes, and once when Sarah was picked up in the middle of winter with snow on the ground someone said:

Q Don't your feet get cold?
A Well ... they get cold at first ... then they get warm.
Q Is there any snow about?
A *Oooooh* ... yes. Yer feet don't touch the bottom ...

Her clothes she said, were 'what they give yuh' but she was fortunate in that the kindly Mrs Roper would 'cut an old skirt down for me', though when it had passed down through the four Roper daughters it was probably in a poor state. But the Ropers could do nothing about shoes, even when the relatively well-off Teresa took over the role of protector.

A I'm not bad off 'cos Teresa give me a good few 'an hers is *nice* clothes.
Q But does she never give you shoes then?
A They don't fit me. She says ... she says ... I haven't got shoe feet ...

It is phrases like 'shoe feet' which crop up constantly and about which Ann Dowling herself has not the faintest idea that add a powerful feeling of authenticity to Sarah's story. One presumes that walking barefoot for years in all weathers had broadened and perhaps deformed the girl's feet so that ordinary shoes just could not be put on. There are, incidentally, several Roper families in the district at the relevant time, but the most interesting is Teresa Roper, a confectioner who in 1843 was at 31 Byrom Street. In 1845 this is run by William Roper and Teresa seems to have vanished – whether to the grave, to a husband or to another man is not known. Sarah always insists that her benefactress married James Wannamaker.

There is a very moving sequence when one Christmas Sarah was found walking through the snow to Mrs Roper's house hoping to get a dinner.

A Mrs Roper sort of minds me ... all of the other step girls have somebody who minds them ... She's a bit better today y'know (*Mrs Roper had been ill*) Oh ... I'm awful glad.
Q What are they going to give you? (*Sarah had arrived and was sitting down*)
A (*in raptures*) Potatoes ... an' (*almost beside herself*) An' gravy ... an' I'll get a wedge an' all. (*Long silence as she apparently looks at the plate in front of her. Then delightedly*) I've got *four* potatoes ... Ummmmmmmm ... I wish I could keep one.
Q What for?
A (*pathetically*) For when I 'aven't got none ...

For much of her early life, Sarah earned a little money and some food by washing
steps at a farthing a time

With her wedges, occasional potatoes and mugs of cocoa, and her cast-off
clothing the little girl struggles through her childhood: more and more she
seems to have slept in the Roper's lobby – and adds a touch that seems most
unlikely to have come from any imagination: 'When it's cold ... I tie me
skirt below me feet with string ... to keep them warm.' Of all what we would
consider deprivations, the only one that really seemed to upset Sarah was
cold: time and time again there is a wistful longing when she talks of
warmth, and almost savours the word as if in uttering it she would feel a
glow. On the way to the Ropers' house at Christmas she had said:

A The houses smell nice ...
Q What do they smell of?
A Waaarm ... smell waaarm. 'Spose that's 'cos everyone has the oven on for
   dinner ...

And again, when she had been talking about the 'posh' houses up the hill:

Q Haven't you ever thought of going there to scrub their steps? They would
   give you money wouldn't they?
A *Oh ... no ...* They have *servants* ...
Q If you asked them nicely they might take you.
A Oh no ... I'd think ... more likely to give you a clip ... they don't even let
   you look ... in the winders no more ... No ... they put shutters up an' you

can't see the fire no more ... (*very wistful*) *Aaah* ... they WAS nice, them fires ...

In the first of Ann's regressions she was, as usual in first sessions, being taken to spot ages to try to build up a broad framework of the personality's life before looking at it in detail. She had been told to come to the age of eighteen, until when she had done little but roam the streets and scrub steps. Sarah said that she was polishing the fender of a certain Wiseman 'the old jewman'. She explained who he was and how she had been forced to seek shelter from the streets: how she kept his house clean and was allowed to sleep in the rags in the basement. His whole character and way of life emerges over a great many regressions in considerable detail, but is probably coloured by prejudices and preconceived ideas so that he stands as something of a Fagin-figure.

A Ooooo ... 'e's 'orrible ... 'e keeps lookin' at yuh ... an' pinches yuh ... on the behind.
Q What do you say when he pinches you?
A He's got awful bony fingers ... an' doesn't half hurt ... 'e's a dirty old man ... an' he looks at yuh ... an' 'e always finds something for yuh to do ... *an'* I'm glad I never liked 'im ...

Sarah never quite resolved the Wiseman/Polish problem mentioned earlier, though almost for the sake of convenience she settled for the first name. He spoke 'funny' she said, and when you asked him something he would say 'Vot ... Vot?' He dressed in a coat with tails and a split up the back – 'Is that so it won't keep you warm?' – and had little things 'like socks' over the tops of his shoes. Out of doors he wore a big hat – 'a top hat with a funny shape at the bottom', but it was his indoor clothing on Fridays that especially fascinated Sarah.

A On Friday night we 'ave to light candles ... an' he goes funny on Friday night.
Q How many candles do you light?
A I think it's seven ... it's a funny shape ... it's aaaah ... like round but it's not round ...
Q Where do you put the candles?
A Well ... do you know a farthing? Well, a farthing's round an' it's like half a farthing ... it's round but it's not round ...
Q What else does he do on Friday night?
A 'E wears 'is 'at.
Q The top hat?
A *Oh no.* An' 'e 'as a shawl ... an' all the people say 'e's an old woman. (*Sarah chuckles at the memory – one of the very rare occasions when she does so*).
Q What colour is this shawl?
A 'S white, an' it's got a lotta sewing on it.

The candles in particular seemed to worry Sarah, who stopped answering questions for a minute to count with her finger the branches as she summoned up an image of the menorah in front of her. 'There's a straight-up one' she muttered to herself, 'an' one … two … three … four … on that side … an' one … two … three … four on that … nine.' Still dissatisfied she counted again and again, sometimes making it nine and sometimes seven, before she abandoned the problem.

The ten years at Wiseman's house saw a gradual and slight up-turn in Sarah's fortunes: she had shelter of a sort, even if she had to pay for it with hard housework, cleaning, blackleading grates and shining fenders, and also the continual bony bottom pinching. Teresa Roper, now Wannamaker, supplied her fairly regularly with clothing – at one ecstatic period she had three dresses. This led to a touching sequence which perhaps gives a wonderful insight into what poverty really means.

Q What's the best thing that has happened to you this year, Sarah?
A Ah … aaaaah … when … I got that frock with the lace on. Teresa gave it to me … *an' you can't see me feet* … no … *no* …

The dress apparently was blue, with lace and buttons down the front, and three-quarter sleeves though Sarah could only describe them as 'They're long an' they're not long'. When asked on what occasions she wore that dress she replied:

A *I don't* … I put it on sometimes when it's night (*almost in tears of happiness*) an' … an' I pretend I'm posh. It's not like the other frocks … it has … petticoat … yuh can't take it out of it.

Asked if she would ever wear it, she said that she would not, but when it was cold she put her feet inside it at night to keep them warm.

In addition to regular clothing her food seemed to have improved. A woman named Sarah who is never properly identified but for whom Sarah Williams seems to do 'some jobs', often gives her hot meals, generally broth: 'but sometimes I have *stew* … it's not like broth … it has potatoes in it an' barley … *an' sometimes* … meat.'

When Sarah was asked if she ever had leftovers from Wiseman's table she snapped with a vehemence and a turn of phrase very unusual for her, and perhaps prompted by her conscious mind: ''E never leaves nothin' … it's a wonder he don't draw 'is breath twice …' This naturally led to questioning Sarah on kosher food.

Q What food does old Wiseman have?
A Oh – he doesn't eat the same as anyone else … he had Jews' food … they have special food for Jews.
Q But what kind of special food?
A They go to a special shop for it an' you can only eat it if you're a Jew.

Sarah talked at some length about Wiseman's religious observances: she said he went to the 'Jews' church' on Saturday – but insisted that he went in a carriage which is most unlikely and that on Friday evenings he put on his little black hat, lit the candles, talked foreign and said that it was new year when it was not. All of this could, of course, be a spill-over from Ann Dowling's present life memory, but it is unlikely that the following extracts could be:

Q Do you know where the one [i.e. church] that Mr Wiseman goes to is?
A Mmmmm … it's not … a road … it's … a … street (*very uncertain*) … it's in Liverpool. I think it's called Hope … [A Synagogue in Hope Place appeared soon after 1836 and was run by the Rev. S. Oppenheim and R. D. Meyer Isaacs.]
Q What do Mr Wiseman's friends do? Do you know any of their names or their jobs?
A One makes furniture … Isaacs … *Isaacs* …
Q And who else comes? What other friends has he got?
A He knows a doctor … ooooooo … it's a funny name … it's a long one … I know 'e's a little fat man … E … E … E … *Epstein* …

There is no trace of a medical man named Epstein at this period, but there certainly was a John Isaacs, a joiner, who lived in Pleasant Street in the 1830s. In the mysterious way in which Sarah seems to get names at least partly correct, is this the man to whom she was referring?

The long sequence directly concerning Wiseman ended with a delightful parthian shot, said in all seriousness by Sarah. As she had mentioned several times in earlier regressions that nuns came to houses asking for money, she was asked:

Q Do these nuns ever knock at Wiseman's door?
A *Oh no* … Cooooooooo. *Oh no* … People don't knock at 'is door … 'e'd charge yuh for knockin'.

The Wiseman period, covering as it did Sarah's teens and early adult life, threw up some interesting material about her private life. As a real person would be, she was now much more fluent and forthcoming than she had been as a small, bewildered step girl, and although in general she tended to be extremely prudish, she was quite free in answering questions on her personal hygiene. She washed, she said, when it was warm, in a bucket in the Roper's yard, drawing water from the pump. She was scandalized at the thought of washing her body all over frequently.

Q How often do you wash your body? Once a week? Once a day?
A *Oh God … no … you'd die.*
Q How often then?
A Maybe two … maybe three … times a year.

Real Reincarnation?   Like a fair proportion of subjects under deep hypnosis, Sarah scratched frequently, though it seemed that in her case it was her head that was itching, rather than the rest of the body. She immediately admitted when asked that she had 'louses' and launched into one of her longer speeches.

A I wash me 'air in a bucket in Mrs Roper's yard ... it's lousy ... got a lotta louses, y'know ... makes me wash it with ... some *ugh* ... smelly ... uh ... burns you right ... in a bottle, but she said it gets rid of all yer louses ... she gave me a comb once so as I wouldn't 'ave louses ... but it got broke ... everybody's got louses.
Q Have the nuns got them?
A That's why they keep their 'eads covered up ...

The synagogue next to the church in Hope Place which Eric Wiseman visited on the Jewish Sabbath

Laundry facilities for Sarah were non-existent, and when she was asked about this she produced one of those strange snippets of historical detail that make this regression so remarkable.

Q When do you wash your dress?
A It just wears out. There's a woman bin round tryin' to make people wash their clothes.
Q Oh? What is her name?
A Kitty …
Q Kitty what?
A She's got two names … I think she's called Wilkin … Wilkinsss … Wilkinson … an' she wants people to get baths.
Q What does she want people to get baths for?
A Well – she says you won't get sick … *But you'll die* … They're opening a place y'know where you can go an' get a bath …
Q Would you go?
A *No.*

There is obviously a memory here – whether of a woman called Sarah Williams or of Ann Dowling's schooldays – of Kitty Wilkinson, the social reformer in Liverpool in the first half of the nineteenth century. Kitty's first husband was lost at sea and although she was desperately poor she devoted herself to good works and urged the setting-up of wash-houses for the poor, limewashing walls and using carbolic acid as a disinfectant in an effort to minimize the fever epidemics that swept through the town every few years. There is no doubt too that it is carbolic acid that Sarah is referring to in the 'smelly … ugh … burns' comment on the treatment of 'louses'. In 1823 the widow Kitty Delmonte married Thomas Wilkinson (is this the inspiration behind Sarah's 'She's got two names … ?') and became more interested in adult literacy. Through her rich patrons she tried to set up reading rooms where those who wished to could learn to read free of charge. Sarah made what is probably a reference to this too in passing: she had been asked the name over a shop, and said that she could not read, then added, 'There's a woman what's teaching people to read … I wish I could read …'

As Sarah was answering so well and was so free from embarrassment in this 'personal' sequence, she was asked:

Q Sarah, can I ask you a rather personal question? What happens to you every month? Does something happen to you every month?
A Mmmmmmmm.
Q Well, what do you call it?
A (*surprised that anyone should not know*) That's called a gift from God.
Q Do you have something special that you wear, or something?
A (*emphatically*) No.
Q Have you ever had a month when you haven't had this gift from God?
A I didn't use to have it when I was little …

A public bath house founded in mid-nineteenth century Liverpool by Kitty
Wilkinson who tried to improve the living conditions of the poor

It was at this stage that more was learned of Teresa Roper and her marriage
to the American. Mr Wannamaker, Teresa's husband, worked for the
government according to Sarah, but unfortunately although the Wanna-
makers were a very powerful and influential family in both commerce and
politics in the nineteenth century there is no record of any of them being in
the United States diplomatic service at this period. If James Wannamaker
did exist, he was probably connected with the many US shipping lines that
had offices in Liverpool. He was, Sarah said, rich and had a carriage, but he
took a dislike to the little girl that Teresa helped – 'because I've got the
mark of the devil on my face'.

There was a strange incident at one regression when an American, Thelma
Palmer, was present. She and Ann Dowling had talked for a long time before
the session began and after twenty minutes – Sarah was talking freely and
cheerfully about polishing Wiseman's fender with a powder from a box –
Thelma asked her first question: 'Is there a name on the box?' Sarah's reaction was instantaneous and frightened: she cowered back in the chair; her
face took on a look of terror; she began panting in a frantic manner and
wringing her hands as she always does when in deep distress. Three times
Keeton asked 'What's the matter, Sarah?' before a faint voice whispered,
'Teresa's ... husband ... talks like ... that'. When awakened she said that
she knew in her head how the word Wannamaker should be pronounced,
but no one in any of the previous regressions had said it correctly. When it
was spoken with an American accent, all the terror of the man flooded back
to her. This fear of the unknown, even if no more than a foreign intonation,
is deep in the basic human personality – probably for sound evolutionary

reasons – and in the closed, stifling and illiterate atmosphere of Sarah's slums it rose to paranoia.

Liverpool, for geographical and historical reasons, has a higher proportion of people of Irish descent than any other city in Britain, and unfortunately a small number brought, and have maintained, their political and sectarian rivalry. And just as in Liverpool one can see a miniature picture of some of the conflicts of Ireland itself, so in Ann/Sarah we can see an even smaller image of the partisan struggles within the city. In the 1840s and '50s when tens of thousands of starving, homeless and pathetic families reduced to utter degradation flooded in, the resentments and fears among the resident population of the town grew very bitter. Basically perhaps the problem was economic – loss of jobs, depressed wages – but as always in such situations it is easier to rationalize feelings and to attack something more tangible – and in this case the Catholic church was an obvious victim.

In Irish-Catholic Ann Dowling's personality as the extreme-Protestant-English Sarah Williams we can see all of the twisted mythology that through the ages has nutured prejudices, purges and pograms. Unquestioningly she believes in and acts on the most outrageous partisan propaganda. When Ann discusses the character after a session she tells those who feel sorry for the pathetic little waif to spare their pity, for running through Sarah is a streak of ruthless toughness, probably born of sheer necessity to survive. She will, for example, terrify the credulous adults of the slum alleys who are unkind to her with her purple birthmark, which was thought to be the mark of the Devil.

The vendetta against the Irish is unremitting at every stage of Sarah's life: a mild outburst at eighteen:

A I don't go to Liverpool now 'cos you gotta go by them Irish … an' they won't let you pass … they call you names … *Oh God … they're everywhere …*

The Irish, according to Sarah were always drunk, always fighting, the men were big, but the women were worse. A typical fight sequence came right in the very first regression and probably has a very strong ring of truth. It concerned what was probably an Orange Day parade when the Protestants, perhaps provocatively, celebrated the Battle of the Boyne under King William III in 1690.

A They 'ad a fight y'know. (*very proudly*) *We won.*
Q When was this? What started the fight?
A It's them with their 'oly water … somebody knocked King Billy off 'is 'orse.
Q Who is King Billy?
A 'E was on 'is 'orse … he's a man what's dressed up … 'an some of the Irish knocked 'im off 'is 'orse … It was King Billy's day … An' there was one of them priests what gets dressed like a nun …
Q And what was he doing?
A 'E was fightin' an' all … then we went over and battered them all up … an' then the policemen came with the … wagon.

Q What's it called?
A They usually call it the body box ... but it's got another name.
Q Was anybody badly hurt in the fight?
A There wasn't nobody dead then, but they was dead after ...
Q Why, what caused that?
A That 'oly water ... they 'it somebody on the 'ead with it.

It is the priests and nuns that come in for the most savage and uncomprehending strictures. Sarah seems utterly confused by the habits and sometimes the priests are described as men dressed like women, but more often
it is the nuns, who Sarah believes are male. On one occasion she describes
monks as having 'no middle to tops of their 'eads'. All of the bigoted
rumour and twisted propaganda comes to the surface.

A ... the nuns live all together in a 'ouse.
Q What do they call it where the nuns live.
A Well ... I've 'eard it called a few names.
Q Come on, tell us what do they call it?
A It's called ... the Witches den an' ... *the whore house.*
Q Why do they call it that?
A 'Cos they say it isn't natural.
Q What isn't natural Sarah?
A Don't know ... must be whore houses that aren't natural.
Q What is a whore house then?
A It's where the nuns live.
Q What is a whore then?
A They go down where the Irish are ...

Nuns, says Sarah, are mucky, knock on doors and take your step money,
have the evil eye, and put curses on people – and to justify the last accusation
she quotes an incident when as a nun looked at a boy in the street a stone fell
from the sky and split his head open.
    It is not only the Catholic church that Sarah finds incomprehensible – the
whole of her little world seen through her limited mind is confusion. On
one occasion she was trying to get a date for a particularly bad winter when
she said the river had frozen over.

Q Do you know what year it was?
A No – all they ever say is it's the year of our Lord ...
Q How old were you then?
A It was when I were twelve.
Q And how old are you now?
A I'm eighteen.
Q So it was six years ago?
A Tha's a long time ... *but it's still the Year of our Lord* an' it was then, an' all,
    y'know. Why is it always His year?

One of the most delightful confusions occurred when the seven-year-old
Sarah was discovered on her way to the Ropers' to have her Christmas dinner
of potatoes and gravy.

A I don't know why it's called Christmas ... (*Long pause, then very tentatively*)
   It's somebody called Jesuses birthday.
Q Who was He?
A I don't know.
Q Hasn't anybody told you about Him at all?
A Oh ... it's 'Is birthday ... But why do they call 'Is birthday Christmas? It
   should be ... Jesusesmas ... Jesusesmas ... that's not right.
Q Well, who was He?
A I don't know but 'E's famous, 'cos everybody 'as a dinner on 'Is birthday.
Q What else do they do at Christmas, Sarah?
A They always shout *Mary Christmas* ... (*very puzzled silence*) *Who's Mary
   Christmas?* (*to herself*) Mary Christmas? Mary Christmas? (*louder*) it's all
   wrong ... why do they say *Mary Christmas* when it's Jesuses birthday?
   Who is Mary Christmas?

Or again, in the middle of a tirade against the Irish she said that they had
stopped fighting because there had been a big procession as an archbishop
had come to visit the city.

A He come on one of them *lo ... co ... mo ... tives*. An' um ... he was (*long
   pause*) it's um ... he's from the Holy See.
Q From the Holy See, is he?
A Um ... don't know where that is.

The opening of the Liverpool and Manchester Railway, 15 September 1830, during
which Walter Huskisson was knocked down and killed

Q What is the Holy See, Sarah?

A I dunno … mus' be a big river somewhere.

In a later regression she suggested that the Holy See or Sea as she envisaged it was where the Holy water came from.

But the most delightful howler occurred when Sarah was talking about the opening of the Liverpool to Manchester railway, the world's first passenger line. As Stephenson's *Rocket* made the first ceremonial procession along the track Walter Huskisson, a Liverpool MP and until the previous year an important cabinet minister, was knocked down and killed as he tried to cross the track to speak to some dignitaries on the opposite side. The incident occurred in 1830 perhaps fifteen years before the time at which Sarah claimed she was talking but no doubt the memory ripples of such an event would be visible for many years later. Sarah had been savouring one of her favourite words – 'Lo … co … mo … tive – that's a lovely word.'

A Some fella got run over wi' one of them, y'know.

Q Did he? Did you know that man's name that got run over by the loco-motive? Was it anybody you knew?

A I didn't know 'im … but 'e was somebody famous … fancy losin' yer ollies when you're famous. [ollies is a local word for marbles.] He was famous … I don't think he lived in Liverpool … he only came to see us … that's why he wasn't lookin'.

Q What was the first letter of his name? Can you remember it?

A He was run over by the very first one …

Q Was he? What *did* his name start with?

A Huh … Hus … Huskins … Huskiss … somethin' like that.

Q That's right … Huskiss?

A *Huskins … it was Huskins … son. (delighted at having found the answer. Then a sudden frown, and almost to herself)* Well … why didn't his dad stop 'im from going in front of the train?

Q Why? Was his dad there as well?

A Well … he musta bin if he was Huskins' son …

It would perhaps be easy to say that Ann Dowling's two recurrent night-mares and her regressions are rather like the English examination essay that asks candidates to write a story that starts with, say, a man standing on an Alpine peak in a thunderstorm, and ends in a prison cell in Bogota. In between Ann's empty room and her death, which arose as just ordinary dreams, there are perhaps sixty marvellous hours of the rambling fantasies of a mind liberated by hypnosis. But unfortunately for this theory, apart from a very rare occasion when a long-dead school lesson might be the source, there seems no physical way in which Ann could have collected the factual material unless memory has in one way or another been transmitted.

And the nightmares themselves? Since the very first regression two years ago there has not been a single recurrence.

4. The Shadow Self

Michael O'Mara

The great psychologist Carl Jung believed that at the gate of the unconscious stood the shadow self – the complete opposite of the conscious personality that everyone sees in our everyday lives. The shadow of the ardent pacifist is the violent sadist; of the shy introvert, the brawling extrovert; of the campaigning moralist, the roué. Past the shadow, deeper into the unconscious, is the anima, or animus in a woman, which is a much more sympathetic element with the characteristics of the opposite sex. Whatever part the unconscious may or may not play in the ultimate explanation of regression, Jung would have been delighted at the number of subjects who seem to vindicate his theory by becoming first a personality of their own sex that they dislike intensely, and then one of the opposite which seems to satisfy some deep need. Often in these cases the second figure is much more vague and shadowy than the first, but perhaps this is no more than a reflection of the fact that the human mind is generally more definite about what it hates than what it loves.

The Shadow Self

Jung would certainly have appreciated a series of regressions by a senior business executive from Philadelphia, Michael O'Mara. As the name suggests, Michael has some Irish ancestry but after three generations in America the Celtic element has become much more diluted than the O'Mara would suggest. His restless driving energy for work, too, appears to owe more to the sterner Puritan ethics of northern Europe than to the gentler Catholicism of Ireland. Even the strictest Protestant moralist, however, would have to admit that no one has seen the effect of drink on Michael – indeed, if there is one thing he despises more than laziness it is drunkenness. It was something of a shock therefore for Michael in his first regression to find himself totally and uncontrollably involved in the character of Stephen Garrett, an idle, drunken layabout in Dublin at the end of the nineteenth century, living rough in stables and alleys, and preoccupied by where the next glass of whiskey, porter or the illegal and lethal poteen was coming from.

As he was moved forwards from his early teens the decay in his personality and faculties became apparent: his speech, which had taken on an increasingly Irish accent as he moved more deeply into the character of Stephen Garrett, assumed not so much the slurring of the casual drunk, but the physical degeneration of the addict. The sharp Irish wit of his younger days dropped into doltish stupidity and then to incoherence as he groped for words hidden somewhere in his drugged and poisoned brain, only to find that he no longer had any control over them, or anything else.

It is an intensely moving experience, swinging from humour to pathos, from innocent wonder to the permanent incoherence of the alcoholic. In a theatrical context it would earn high praise for the acting, and the script has all the relentlessness of great Greek tragedy, with inexorable Fate driving the weak, thriftless yet basically harmless Stephen to his own wretched destruction. It is one of the finest-drawn character studies of the regressions in this book, and although positive facts such as names and dates are rare, the atmosphere and circumstantial evidence builds up a very telling and impressive case of the desperate condition of Ireland at the end of the nineteenth century. In sixty years over four million people – half the total population of 1840 – had emigrated, mainly to England or America, and of those that remained fifty-five per cent were what one yearbook of 1901 euphemistically described as 'indefinite or non-productive in occupation'. Bad potato harvests in the last decade of the century increased the grinding poverty which made the bitter political struggle for independence more savage. In its turn this brought more repression, more troops, and in this world of semi-starvation and unemployment, soul-destroying even for the best, what chance was there for a pathetic and inadequate lad, probably illegitimate and orphaned early?

It is difficult to deal with the life of the character Stephen Garrett in a strict chronological order as can be done with most subjects because apart from one very moving sequence as a small child and another at his death at about the age of twenty-seven, his story is a confused blur with little to mark the passage of time except a steady degeneration. Drink dominates much of

Poole Street, Dublin, *c.* 1900. This is typical of the poverty at the turn of the century to which Stephen refers

his conversation, but as might be expected from a homeless, penniless outcast, food, shelter, clothing and avoiding work and the police figure fairly prominently on his hazy horizon.

At first it was assumed that the opening sequences were blurred and muttered in the way typical of many early regressions, but as it continued long after things should have become clearer the suspicion of drunkenness crept in. No real hint of date or place could be obtained, but Michael's lips obviously became dry as he licked them constantly.

Q What *is* your name?
A (*sighs weakly and indistinctly*) Thirsty ...
Q Here you are ... drink this. How's that? [There was no actual movement on the part of either questioner or subject during the exchange.]
A (*with sudden vehemence and disgust*) Ugggggggh ... That's water.
Q What did you expect? What drink were you expecting?
A (*faintly and wearily again*) Uh ... um ... on'y a drink ...
Q What do you usually drink? What is your favourite drink?
A (*pause*) Any ... kind ... drink.
Q Why do you want a drink?
A Thirsty.

Q Is there any reason for being thirsty?
A Wanna ... drink.
Q Is it hot? Is that why you want a drink?
A Dry ...
Q Is it because you are ill you want a drink?
A Um ... no.
Q Is it because you are afraid you want a drink?
A (*sudden flash of annoyance*) *No* ... It's because I'm dry I want a drink.

No doubt this illogical reasoning seemed convincing to the personality that later emerged as Stephen Garrett, but it confirmed to the questioners that he was drunk, though whether it was any more than a temporary lapse, no one knew at that time. On a good many occasions Edna Greenan as Nell Gwynn was found incoherently babbling and completely intoxicated, but moved forwards or backwards a few hours she became perfectly sober and normal.

Whether it was the effect of the imaginary drink of water or not, Stephen slowly became rational enough to give a brief outline of himself at that moment and some idea of the lines along which the regression was to develop – the humour, the pathos, the bewilderment.

Q How are you dressed? Look down at yourself. [A question which can sometimes give a clue to period or lead to a line of questioning.]
A (*pause*) My trousers are not very nice.
Q What is the matter with them?
A Ripped ... they're comic.
Q Ripped, are they? What *is* your name?
A Dunno.
Q Do you know which town you are in?
A Uhuh ... it's a city.
Q A city is it? Are there many cars about?
A Oh no. There aren't many cars about.
Q But you do know what a car is, though?
A Yeh.

This seemed to indicate that the date was well into the twentieth century, but in the event the question backfired in a way it did on several occasions with Michael's regressions. When later it seemed evident that Stephen's period was in the 1890s, cars in the Dublin streets seemed the one glaring anachronism in what was otherwise a regression remarkably consistent in accuracy of timing. As it was very early in the first session it was assumed that the conscious mind had temporarily broken through: several months later, however, Stephen was suddenly asked how many wheels a car had, and without a moment's hesitation answered 'Two'. When asked what made it go he replied with a touch of scorn 'Horse', and it was then realized that he must have been referring quite genuinely to the Irish jaunting car, and not an automobile.

From now on Michael's voice took on progressively an accent different from his educated East Coast American: it was not the incomprehensible slang and pronunciation of the Dublin slums which the original Stephen would probably have used, but what is generally accepted as 'Irish' in entertainment. He was, he said, standing in a street by a bridge.

Q What is the bridge over? What do you see if you look down?
A River.
Q What is the name of the river? You have been standing there … you know the name of the river.
A Oh … it's … a … it's [In a later regression he mentioned the name Liffey correctly in answer to the same question]
Q What kind of bridge is it?
A It's just … like the street … cobbled … it's a … very wide street. The bridge has got … it's a rail … made of stone … and things that go like that (*mimes a typical baluster*) … an' there's hundreds of 'em …
Q And what is on the other side of the bridge?
A The street goes on … up a hill.

The photograph of O'Connell Bridge taken in the early 1900s fits Stephen's description exactly. In one regression he hesitantly named O'Connell Street

This photograph of O'Connell Bridge shows how accurate Stephen's description was. Irish jaunting cars can be seen near the statue

when pressed, but did not seem very sure about it, probably because when he claimed to have lived it was officially called Sackville Street though O'Connell was an alternative used in certain circles.

It soon became obvious that Stephen had no job and was living rough in stables and alleyways – a young man of the street – and he was asked about his relations with the police.

Q Have you ever been in the hands of the police?
A May … be … I have.
Q How did they catch you?
A (*amused snort*) Ha … I think I might ov bin a bit obvious … [the first flash of the occasional dry humour that made his regressions delightful]
Q Picking pockets?
A *No.*
Q Stealing from stalls at the side of the road?
A Jus' food.
Q When you had this brush with the police, what uniforms did they wear?
A (*dubiously*) I … think … a … grey hat.
Q Was it tall or flat?
A Some of them were … (*in a rush*) there … were two kinds … but they had big belts.

Round police helmets were worn by the Irish Constabulary

Q Did they threaten to use them on you?
A No ... *Nooo* ... they just held their fat guts in.

As the illustrations show there were two types of police helmet in use in Ireland at the time, probably those of the Royal Irish Constabulary, who operated mainly in the rural areas, and the Metropolitan Police in Dublin.

In any regression it is important to check the accuracy of known events, topography, people and domestic details which the subject is describing before attaching too much significance to his personal life and feelings, which cannot usually be verified. In view of this Stephen was questioned further on his home city which he named at last as Dublin.

Q Go over the bridge and tell me what shops there are ... the first one.
A It's ... a ... pub ... on the right side ... a black sign.
Q What is on the sign?
A It's red ... a red ... red words.
Q Can you read them?
A No.
Q What is the picture then?
A It's a ... red thing ... it's like ... a like ... like a ... chess thing. [On being wakened Michael drew a crude pawn, but whether the sign was actually

The Land League, however, wore tall police helmets

a chess piece or whether he had misinterpreted the drawing it is difficult to say.]

Q What is the first real shop then?
A It's a ... a tea shop. No ... it's ... No ... it's not a ... you ... go in there an' they pour it out for yuh ... eat ... eat a tea ... You go in there an' get a tea-an'-eat.
Q What would they charge you for a tea-and-eat?
A Uhuh ... I wouldn't know that.
Q If you paid, what would you pay in?
A Huh ... ah ... if ... well ... pennies.

In a slightly more lucid, though still not very coherent moment Stephen was taken back to the O'Connell Bridge and asked about ships:

Q What are the big ones like down at the mouth of the river?
A Um ... they got ... ah ... there's a ... well ... thing on the side. (*long pause as Stephen groped for a description and made vague circular motions with his hand*) a thing on the side ... like a windmill thing.
Q A windmill thing?
A The windmill thing goes round ... and the ship ... disappears.
Q And what makes the windmill go round? The wind?
A Uh ... ha ... *Nooo ... nooooo*. The wind pushes the sails, which is ... I think makes the ship go ... it's ... a ... the ... there's some kind of a ... well ... there's *something* there that makes the dam' thing go.

The illustration shows how the quay to which Stephen was referring looked in 1880 when the great majority of ships were driven by sails. The evidence of the regression suggests that he lived ten to fifteen years later when although the scene would look much the same there would have been a large increase in the number of steam-powered vessels. To the casual and probably slightly intoxicated viewer the propeller-driven boats, which in a small port would still be largely wooden, would look very much like sailing ships, whereas the paddle steamers with their huge whirling, splashing wheels would make a deep impression, as they obviously did on Stephen.

On another occasion when an observer very familiar with Dublin was present Stephen was asked if he had ever been down where 'the big ships are' and when he said he had, he was asked to describe the journey from the city centre. He gave a remarkably accurate picture of the embankment and the terraces of elegant Georgian houses with their pale brick and tall windows.

Q Are there any particular buildings there where the ships are?
A There's a big ... castle ... *no* ... it isn't a castle ... it's like a castle.

This seems almost certainly to be the famous Custom House which was built at the end of the eighteenth century.

Custom House Quay. The ship with 'the windmill-thing' or paddle on the side can be seen in the foreground

The obsessional craving of the dypsomaniac is brilliantly portrayed in Michael O'Mara's regressions: wherever Stephen is taken, apart from the short excursion into childhood, the question of drink arises sooner or later. In the early part of the first regression when nothing definite had been established about the character, Keeton made one more attempt to find a name.

Q What *is* your name? You must have a name: what is it?
A Uh … uh … Stephen? (*more confidently*) Stephen … Stephen.
Q Do you have another name? Don't they call you mister something?
A (*derisive snort*) *Ha! They do not.*
Q What would they shout if they wanted you to come?
A (*again snorts in derision*) *Ha!* They wouldn't want me to come … they'd want me to go … I'm thirsty.
Q Well, here's a bar. What would you like to drink?
A Porter … *Aaaaaah.* Porter. *Aaaaaaaw.* That's a nice (*pause and mimes drinking*) drink …
Q Would you like something short afterwards to chase it down?
A You got it backwards.
Q What would you like?
A (*very emphatically*) Whiskey.
Q Any particular brand? There are lots of brands here?
A No … uh … jus' whiskey … Irish … that's whiskey.

Porter is the old name for the very dark and heavy beer more generally known as Guinness or stout: it was immensely popular in the nineteenth century especially among working men, particularly in Ireland. It is a word which Michael would never use in his waking state, though he was vaguely aware that it was some kind of beer. When he was brought round he said how much he had physically enjoyed the taste of the porter, which he could actually feel going down his throat.

On another occasion someone mentioned poteen, the illicit and notorious spirit made in Ireland from almost any material available.

Q Do you like poteen, Stephen?
A Poteen? (*slowly*) I ... do ... not ... like ... it.
Q Why not? I should have thought you would be very fond of it.
A (*very deliberately with the pseudo dignity of the half-drunk*) People ... who drink that stuff ... they got ... I mean ... they got hair comin' outa their feet. An' they don' wear shoes ... an' it's jus' as well ... 'cos they couldn't afford 'em, anyway.
Q What do you drink Stephen?
A *Oooooh* ... jus' beer, y'know ... I don' mind ... too bad.
Q Where do you get your beer?
A In the pub.
Q Which pub?
A (*again with alcoholic dignity*) I ... understan' ... a number of them ... serve it.

Although it was difficult to judge Stephen's real age, it seemed that the extract above was from his late teens: in his mid-twenties he had degenerated, and the slightly amusing antics of the drunk had become rather sordid.

Brewing home-made poteen under difficulties. As alcoholism took a grip, Stephen grew to like the poteen he had once disdained

He was brought forward five years from the previous incident, and his face which had been relaxed, tightened into genuine pain. He said that he had been drinking with three friends and

A I mus' ah … uhuh … O Chris' … I fell over … I don' know what … what the hell happened.
Q Where were you exactly?
A (*long agonized pause … holds forehead, very upset*) Uh … ah … ah … ah. Yeh … It's an empty place … jus' bare boards … oh … cold … oh … it was there … we jus' had this stuff … whatisname … it's … it's … it's three … lots of us … was sittin' … and we had this … this … (*slowly and with intense feeling*) *Desprit stuff*. Don' know what happened to them.
Q Were they your friends?
A (*groaning and holding forehead again*) Oh God … coulda bin divils. Oh God. I can't even remember who they were … Musta fallen in the stuff … haven't gotta throat left.

There was no doubt that at that moment Stephen was going through the realities of the hangover of all time, and though when Michael was wakened he felt only the usual dryness and taste, under hypnosis he was extremely ill. His eyeballs ached; his head throbbed as if it would burst at the slightest movement; and his throat seemed raw and lacerated as if he had been swallowing acid.

Towards the end of his life Stephen had gone so far that he now enjoyed the poteen he had once disliked so much. He was again being questioned by the Dubliner.

Q What about poteen?
A Iss … not … not bad … but that other stuff … Chris' … it won't go pas' your mouth.
Q What other stuff is that?
A Isss … white … an' red … an' then it's pink.
Q Is it called red biddy?
A (*snort, half-amused, half-derisory*) *Ha*. There's a woman called Red Biddy … great fat woman … you can see her in the dark.

He refused to elaborate on why one could see Red Biddy in the dark – whether it was her bulk, her alcoholic complexion or her profession – but another observer had a very interesting comment to make on the drink of that name. It was, he said, a mixture of port wine (or occasionally whiskey) and methylated spirits, which in the nineteenth century was colourless and free from the unpalatable naphtha. With the cheap, dark-red port in the bottom of the glass and the colourless meths on top, this could well have been the red-white-pink mixture that Stephen described. Certainly there can be no doubting its lethal properties. Not unexpectedly, Michael had not the slightest knowledge of the name Red Biddy or of a drink made from meths and port in his waking state, and was absolutely astounded when he heard Stephen talking about it.

In a late regression when Stephen had been more fluent than usual he was asked about the state of the country because so many important events were taking place, and so many famous figures were striding across the unhappy stage of Irish politics that it was felt that something must have penetrated even the sodden mind of the drunk.

From the point of view of hearing specific names and incidents the sequence was, however, a disappointment, but we must always remember that if the Stephen character was ever a real person he was illiterate, probably of very low intelligence, a solitary and, for much of the time, fuddled with drink. His ambitions were not to see Ireland independent, but to feel Stephen full, warm and drunk. His ideas of the state of the country are probably typical of the emotional and stereotyped generalizations that filter through to the very bottom of the social order – the hazy and resentful rumours that agitators whip up into the frenzy of 'them' against 'us'. Understandably he rejected any knowledge of the Irish Volunteers (formed in 1908), but less understandably he said he knew nothing of Sinn Fein (1902) and rejected the names of the political leaders put to him one after another.

He did have some strong feelings about the English, though.

Q Has anything been happening lately, Stephen?
A Oh ... it's terrible ... *Terrible*. There's no ... it's a *miserable* time.
Q Why?
A Uh ... the people on the street ... Nuthin' ... beggars.
Q Why?
A There ... it's ... all the people are leavin' ... they're going ...
Q Has there been a famine or something?
A There's not enough of anythin' about ... in this country ... There's not even many people left now ... an' them that are lef' ... are all on the street.
Q Is it worse than it was say ten years ago ... or better?
A Oh ... ah ... it's ... no ... *No* ... You can't get worse than dead terrible ... an' that's what it's bin ever since I've known it.
Q Where do the people go when they leave?
A Oh ... they go to England.
Q Have you ever thought of going across there?
A No ... *No.* (*bitterly*) There's enough of the buggers here.

Several times Stephen was brought back to the bitterness and violence that was tearing Ireland apart at the turn of the century. Although some of the worst injustices had been settled, the terrible unemployment problem, the emigration which was still running at about 40,000 a year and the desperate poverty made the whole situation highly explosive, so that there was a very large military presence in the country. The regular army was, however, normally used as a symbol of power or in emergencies, and the day-to-day implementation of the rather repressive laws left to the semi-military Royal Irish Constabulary.

Q Who is supposed to be ruling the country? Who is in charge?
A It's a … it's … uh … generals or something like that … it's all these … soldiers. They're the ones that run the country.

One always sensed that the character Stephen was very ill at ease on the several occasions he was questioned on the political situation, perhaps because there was a very positive conscious-unconscious conflict in these sequences. Michael read politics and history at Temple University, Philadelphia, and though he did not study the period in depth he was familiar enough with the troubles of Ireland in the nineteenth century and with the major figures who fought for independence. The conscious Michael O'Mara could have given a brief outline of the Home Rule problem and of the careers of Parnell, Redmond and O'Connell – all names that Stephen refused to recognize when he was asked. Stephen too was aware of the massive emigration, but insisted that everyone was going to England. Michael knew very well that three-quarters of them went to the USA but in practice almost all came to England first before sailing across the Atlantic from Liverpool. When he was brought back to a waking state Michael said that the names of all of the politicians and leaders of the opposing parties were screaming in his mind, but nothing would induce Stephen to utter them because it seemed that they meant nothing to him.

Although in the political sequences Stephen keeps up a steady sniping at the English there never seems a great deal of venom in his insults – they are almost the routine and unthinking parrot chatter typical of so many members of protest and political movements. But a very real bitterness does creep into his voice when he talks of what he sees as traitors and quislings.

Q Anything happening in Dublin this year? What is the talk about?
A There's a lotta people goin' on about … whatsit … these … English … but they – it's the Irish ones that are my problem.
Q What do the Irish ones want?
A Oh … the usual … they want more money … they want to be the *big* fellas.
Q What do the English want?
A They want to be still the big fellas … they like it. There's no difference.
Q Do you think you will get rid of the English?
A Aw … no … You'll never get rid of the English.
Q Why?
A Well, look. You see, *these* English … tha's only a bit of them … you got England full of 'em … an' the minute you act up, they'll be over on us … There's not many Irish people … England's a big … a bloody … a big place. It's full of 'em over there.
Q Do they ever shoot the Irish?
A *Well* … it's not just the English shoot the Irish … it's more the Irish

shoot the Irish ...
Q Which Irish shoot the Irish?
A (*savagely, with complete contempt*) Well ... I ... they ... I give you they're workin' for the English ... but they're *Irish* ... and *they* shoot the Irish ...

Stephen was only too glad to slip out from this uncomfortable questioning into the more familiar field of his own pathetic plight – though there is never a trace of self-pity in his personal life. Like a number of other characters, especially Sarah Williams, the Liverpool orphan, he bears no resentment against society, and accepts with resignation – or indifference – the fact that he is generally cold, hungry, homeless and an outcast. No more than an animal does he feel bitterness that others have good clothes, regular money and security. Before the following extract he had been describing quite un-emotionally how he slept where he could in empty houses or ruined buildings, and had been living on bread handed out by a lady. He appeared to be slightly drunk.

Q Are you a vagrant?
A (*with alcoholic dignity*) I ... am ... no ... such ... thing.
Q What do you do? You say you do not work for a living and have no home?
A Iss no' ... isss ... not ... easy, y'know.
Q What isn't easy?
A Well ... when ... there's no trade ... an' yuh haven't gotta trade, where are yuh?
Q What trade was your father?
A (*tartly*) Whatever trade it was, 'e's practising it somewhere else now.
Q What about your mother?
A (*an instant and softer tone, quite unexpected, appeared for the first time in the regression*) She's ... she's ... gone. She's ... uhuh ... dead.
Q How old were you when your mother died?
A Jus' small ... small.
Q Who looked after you when your mother died?
A Nobody.
Q (*very gently and sympathetically*) Have you never really worked at anything?
A (*brittle again*) Stayin' alive.
Q Do you remember living anywhere other than in the corner of a stable?
A (*suddenly dreamy and happy, talking softly to himself and quite oblivious of any questioner. A happy smile flickering round his mouth*) It's ... iss. like a nest ...
Q Do you –
A It's like a bird's nest ... (*almost ecstatic*) iss round ... an' warm ... an' you get in the middle ...

This strangely beautiful flash with its dream-like quality, so untypical of Stephen's drunken incoherence or his sharp cynicism, was to appear twice more in the long regression, once as the first thing he remembered when his mother was alive, and once as his last thoughts. But for the moment he seemed almost ashamed at having lowered his guard to let some poetic streak emerge and was glad of an excuse to slide off into more general topics:

Q Do you tend to help yourself if people do not give you things?
A Help myself? We *all* need to help ourselves ... there's no one else lookin' after you.
Q Do you steal from time to time?
A (*with complete sincerity – throughout Stephen insists that he is not a criminal*) I *wouldn't* steal ... I *couldn't* do that ... I'll always look for charity ...

It was a good thing for Stephen and the thousands like him that there was the Victorian upper-class pastime of slumming, do-gooding and providing food for the poor 'who are ever with us'. There was the bread from 'a nice lady' who stood by the bridge, unspecified food from the nuns occasionally, and when his welcome had not been worn out, from a soup kitchen run by some English ladies.

A They give yuh a bowl o' somethin' ... hot water probably.
Q What do they give you to go with it?
A Oh – they give yuh a piece o' bread.
Q What is it like when you go in?
A There's a big ... there's this woman ... she's with the apron ... a big dam' thing ... you *go* in ... you get this thing ... there's a man hands you a piece of bread (*mimicking in a sanctimonious whine*) 'God bless you'.
Q Have you *ever* worked?
A (*slowly, emphatically and with complete candour*) Noo. Well ... there was a time of not wantin' to try, an' now I've got to the time of not being ABLE to try ...

As nothing of Stephen's life had been explored before his teens when he was already a steady drinker, suddenly in the middle of one of his most incoherent and unhappy sequences Keeton broke in the questioning with 'Deep sleep ... deep sleep, Stephen ... Go back to the age of six ... You are six years old ... bring out all the memories of Stephen at the age of six ... Where are you?' Instantly there was a change of facial expression: the drawn and haggard face of the cold, starving and almost delirious Stephen vanished, and the features became relaxed and happy. His voice took on immediately an almost childish quality, and became fluent, clear and without any of the hesitation that characterized so much of the older Stephen's regression. He was, he said, in a park, playing in the grass: there was another child and a 'nice lady' but she was not his mother – she had been there when he arrived.

Mother seemed to be absent much of the time: on some occasions she sold flowers, on others she cleaned houses, according to Stephen. As no mention of a father could be obtained it seems possible the boy was illegitimate and that 'Ma's' commercial activities may not have been entirely connected with floristry or domestic work. In any case she seems to have disappeared early in his life for he is always very hazy about her, and obviously does not remember her clearly. In one of his more lucid moments he says that no one looked after him when his mother died as he had no relatives, though in another regression he mentioned a big sister, but she and 'Ma' seem to have been the same person.

When Michael was wakened he said that he could see the street very clearly under hypnosis, but in the characteristic manner of subjects under regression did not describe it because no one asked him. It was, he said, a long street of three-storey terraced houses with a low wall in front, surmounted by iron railings: at one end was a cemetery and, at the other, a main road. The houses seemed rather grand for the family circumstances, but Michael said that he felt that he and 'Ma' lived in a basement only, which seems much more likely. Certainly the Garrett standard of living did not seem very high:

Q What do you like to eat best, Stephen?
A Yummmm ... (*pause*) Piece o' bread ... an' *sweet* (*face breaks into broad smile of pleasure at the thought*)
Q Some sweet stuff on it?
A Mmmm. Sweet on it.
Q What colour was the sweet stuff?
A (*excited*) Red ...

It is interesting to note that the questioner quite pointedly used the phrase 'sweet stuff' twice, but Stephen rejected it emphatically as if 'sweet' was the word he used for jam.

Wandering through the streets or playing in the park with anyone who happened to be there for much of the day, or sitting as he seemed to be so often 'on the wall waiting for Ma to come home', Stephen must have been a rather lonely little boy, and his life aimless and dull. The dreariness of his existence is highlighted very clearly when a chance question on whether he went to church immediately filled his voice with wonder and excitement. There is no mistaking the sheer joy and delight in this sequence: half a lifetime of adult restraint in displaying emotion vanishes, and Stephen's whole being bursts with wonder, awe and feeling.

Q Has your mother ever taken you to church? Did you go last Sunday?
A Ummm ... I've bin to church ... Um ... ah ... (*suddenly pathetically wistful*) Holdin' the hand ... *it's big* ...
Q Is it the Catholic church or the English church?
A It's not the English church. It's like that ... (*mimes a dome*) It's got a big thing ... with railings round ... high up ... there are glasses *an'* they got pictures on ... (*really excited*) *an'* they *sing* ... the people sing ... people sing ... up in the top.

Q Do you know what they sing?

A They sing ... they sing ... *songs (absolutely delighted)* They sing ... they sing. *(hums something it has not been possible to identify) All at once* ... an' then ... an' then they get ... *there's a thing* [Possibly he is thinking of the organ as taken through the sequence later on he refers to it as 'a machine'] an' *they all sing* ... I don't know the songs. It's nice ... it's ... ah ... p *(word lost) it's real* ... there's big things and big ... seats ... an' all the people in there.

Q Can you see the priest?

A He's got ... the big gold thing hung down his back ... right ... an' it's got a cross *(mimes)* like that.

Q Can you see his back? Can you ...

A *(interrupting and almost ecstatic)* Oooooooh ... it's beautiful.

Q What is he saying?

A Well, he's standing looking up at the front ... an' there's two other ... kids ... who ... they ... *(overcome with awe)* He's got this big thing that comes out like that *(mimes)* ... an' a thing on his head ... an' a big gold thing goin' down his back ... an' a dress. *There's just his feet comin' outa the bottom.*

Q But can you tell what he is saying?

A Well ... he's ... they just talk to each other.

Whatever is operating here, from reincarnation to the unconscious memory, there is no doubt that the mature, professional and widely experienced business executive is actually recreating through the eyes, speech, mentality and gesture, the experience of a small, astonished and overwhelmed little boy. The incoherence here is not the stupidity of alcohol, but the sheer inability to express the emotions that surged through him. It is true that the church has spent nearly two thousand years creating a ritual which does induce these feelings, but for most church-goers the experience was in their earliest days and long forgotten. If hypnosis has no supernatural element and involves only this present existence, it is not less astounding that it can wipe out in an instant a whole lifetime of habit and outlook, and make us experience again for a short while the world through a completely different personality.

The totally convincing childlike innocence that characterizes the church sequence is very evident again when he was asked about his playthings.

Q Do you ever play marbles?

A *(pause: a groping in the recesses of memory, and then a sudden revelation as if an old man had recalled something he had forgotten for half a century)* Marbles! Marbles! *(face wreathes in a smile)* Marbles – you can do that. *(flicks an imaginary marble with finger and thumb delightedly)*

Q How many did you have?

A *(still excited)* A ... a ... big one ... *(words tumble out in a headlong flow)* You get the big one an' throw it an' knock the little ones out an' then you get the little ones an' go like that an' knock the other little ones out an' when you've knocked all the little ones out ... you've won.

79

This seemed to exhaust the childhood memories, for though he was taken back to the period several times, little more emerged except the mother/sister confusion.

To see what happened to the family, Stephen was brought to the age of twelve and at once the face became drawn and miserable. When at last he answered his voice was absolutely dead as he mumbled, apparently with weakness and wretchedness. Much of the sequence was inaudible, but it was learned that he was leaning against the wall of an alley which ran 'behind the English church' – presumably one of the two Protestant cathedrals in Dublin. He was cold, wet and desperately unhappy. 'Gotta get somewhere outa the wet ... an' a bit warm,' he mumbled. One caught a glimpse of the pathetic brotherhood of outcasts, starving, cold, and homeless:

A Ah ... um ... there's ... a ... one of the other ... one of these ladies ... will give me something ... but she's got to get some ... some ... if she ... she gets some maybe she'll get me some too.
Q Where will ...
A She's ... she doesn't have any. No. She's getting some now ... she went ... if she comes in here I'll get some.

The voice became too weak, and Stephen was brought on to eighteen: there was no doubt that he was well on the road to being a permanent drunk. Stumbling confusion dominated the conversation, of which the following is typical:

A There can be ... yeh ... there's a ... horses here ... horses pullin' a ... there's a man comin' ... thing comin' ... four horses ... pullin' it ... 's gotta ... go' come ... uh ... boxes in it ... 's green ... four horses ...

There seemed no point in pursuing the sequence as it was completely incoherent, and as with all subjects, he was brought to his last day: instantly extreme distress was apparent. His head moved painfully from side to side and his left hand made feeble plucking movements at his leg, which was held rigidly in front of him and seemed to be causing intense pain. The speech in this sequence was slurred, incoherent and often inaudible, and seemed to be the rambling of delirium rather than drunkenness.

Q Where are you Stephen?
A Oooooooah. (*groans*)
Q What is the matter?
A Tsssssssss ... can't ... aaaaah.
Q What can't you do?
A Whatacan ... legs ... (*several words unintelligible*) Can't get outa this ...
Q Out of what?
A This thing.
Q Is it a bed?

A *Aaaaaah* … I can' see … it's … a … ah … naw … it's like that … wooden thing … got me in it.

Q Why can't you get out of it?

A I'm stuck.

Q Who put you there?

A *Them buggers*. Down there … they got me in this … they think I'm a criminal.

Q And are you?

A *(with unexpected violence)* I'm no criminal *(whining pathetically again)* I was … just … in the way and I shoulda bin outa the way an' somebody got me … I feel terrible … they've got me. *(rest of the sentence incoherent)*

The whole conversation and the action seemed like some sober Kafkaesque nightmare: Stephen raved in delirium of falling into the road 'by that big bank thing … up Grafton', and being picked up by the police. He kept repeating that he was in the way and he should not have been, and how he could not move his leg which seemed to be sticking out at a strange angle. He raved of a trial before a lord but did not know on what charge: he was rushed in, he said, and everything had been decided before he came. He was carried below and strapped to a framework and beaten by 'the fat bugger with the stick' before being left alone, shivering and aching. All the time the left leg was held rigid and immovable.

On three different and widely separate occasions Michael was taken

Grafton Street with the 'big bank thing' in the background

through this episode, and from hints the reality of the situation – if there is any reality – was that he had been knocked down in Grafton Street, possibly by a cart, and left lying in the bitterly cold, wet street. He seems to have been picked up by police or some other uniformed people, and taken to a hospital or institution dying of a combination of shock, starvation and alcoholism. The being strapped down, the flogging, the brutal guards, the cell, all seem to have been the drugged torments of a dying mind, perhaps with a narcotic to ease the pauper's passing. Once in his agonized hallucinations there came a brief wistful flash:

Q *Is* it a gaol you are in Stephen?
A (*long pause*) Looks … like it … there's a window … up on the wall, an' there's bars … (*pause, then much weaker but almost happily*) an' … an' the sky … the sky's outside …

Stephen was then told to come to the last moments he remembered in his life, which it seemed could not have been long after the last extract. Instantly the anguish disappeared from his face, and the shaking which had persisted throughout the sequence ceased. After a few moments of dead silence, Stephen began the very low gentle humming that had been heard in the church when he was six.

Q (*very softly, as if in the presence of a real death*) What are you humming? Are you singing a song?
A (*a fleeting snatch of a song, too brief to identify and only just audible*) Tssssssssss … (*Humming again, then a pause*) … I wasssssssss thinking … like a little baby … (*hums a few more notes*) Warm … aaah … it's warm … (*A strange expression, half-wonder, half-peace, filled Stephen's face.*)
Q Are you warm?
A Mmmmmmmmm.
Q Are you happy?
A Issssall right … got the covers … (*wearily and weakly mimes pulling up the bedclothes*) … iss all … right now … (*A brief pause, and then the almost inaudible toneless chant again*) an' the sun … is … comin' … right down there … an' … nice … ah now … aaaah … tsssssss.

As the last sibilant faded into silence his head fell forwards – the personality that had been Stephen had gone, and the personality that is Michael was lost in some strange limbo, incapable of speech or action in its own right yet able to respond a minute later to Keeton's instructions:

Q It is five years since the death of Stephen Garrett: you have complete memories of who you are and where you are. What are you doing?

The life of Emmy – the only female character ever assumed by a male in any of Keeton's regressions – was so brief and so vaguely drawn, as might be expected from a sheltered six-year-old of a middle-class family, that little in the way of positive and verifiable facts were produced, and much of its impact rests in the way the 'feeling' of the first years of the century is re-created. Short and sketchy though the regression is there emerges a delicately drawn picture of a rather delightful child as clearly part of the period as a Kate Greenaway drawing. If Emmy sometimes appears to be a little precious, it is the fault of her Edwardian upbringing which tried at the same time to force children to grow up beyond their years and yet to remain quaint and amusing babies.

In the context of hypnosis it was remarkable how Michael changed instantly and completely from the drunken and sometimes brittle Stephen to the coy, yet spontaneous little girl. The vague and trembling mime of the older Stephen became precise and uninhibited as Emmy poured out her imaginary tea or lifted the hem of her dress to show off the edging. Although it seems unlikely that the vocal chords of the average adult male could create the actual sounds of a six-year-old girl, the speech patterns, the gestures and the general personality that was projected almost made those present unaware that the pitch of the voice was an octave or more too low.

That the visual and personality elements contributed so strongly to this impression becomes evidence when one finds that the tape recordings of this session do not convey the child quite so readily.

While Jung's shadow-anima theory of the unconscious fits the two characters of Michael O'Mara so perfectly it does not explain how the character of Stephen, in particular, acquired some of the relatively obscure material that made him into a real person.

Taken one by one many of the 'facts' presented can be explained away in purely rational, normal terms: the Irish accent and turn of phrase, for example, could be dismissed on the grounds that Michael must be very familiar with the stock Irishman of the cinema, TV and radio, and that Stephen uses this rather than the incomprehensible speech of a Dublin slum seems to strengthen the idea. The character mentions only two of the Dublin streets he must have wandered endlessly for years: when asked for names he produced Grafton Street and O'Connell Street – thoroughfares which are as well-known to people who have never visited Ireland as are Fifth Avenue, Piccadilly Circus, the Champs Elysées or Princes Street to those who have never been to New York, London, Paris or Edinburgh.

Even with explanations one feels that the law of averages must apply, and that sooner or later there must be a 'No' to a purely rational explanation. To convince the majority of people, however, a regression must check out historically, and here Michael presents the usual two conflicting aspects – the facts he must know as his twentieth-century self but which he cannot produce under hypnosis, and those which it seems he is unlikely to know yet which he spoke through the mouth of Stephen. The inability to give the political details and names which were hammering through Michael's brain has already been mentioned, and there were many social and personal aspects similarly blocked.

Are our expectations wrong? Do we feel that an illiterate, homeless and dull youth in the slums of the nineteenth century should be able to reproduce the values and attitudes of the late twentieth century? The whole material situation has changed so radically in less than a hundred years: the drop-out of today would find it hard to escape the batterings of the media in one form or another, and even if only hazily and uncomprehendingly would have some idea of today's major issues and personalities. Are we really looking through the unbelievably limited eyes of a pathetic social outcast, or are we again watching the antics of that guardian in the unconscious deliberately playing stupid to prevent its own ignorance of the facts being revealed?

The information which Michael does not know, but which Stephen does, seems to begin with his surname. The character had struggled to recall this in the first three regressions, and it was not until the fourth that it came out 'Garrett … *Garrett*' in a tone which implied 'Why couldn't I get that earlier?' A fantasizing unconscious would most likely have picked one of the standard Irish names – an O'Reilly, a Murphy or a FitzGerald, perhaps – but although Garrett is a very typical surname from Ireland, it is not one that springs readily to mind. Michael says that he does not remember ever having met anyone of that name in his life, and once more, he was completely surprised when he heard himself uttering it. In the first three sessions he had tried desperately to bring out something lurking in the back of his mind, but it would not come: it was only when caught by an out-of-context question that the word surged through.

Stephen's description of O'Connell Bridge is very accurate: '… it's wide … with stones on the street … an' stone railings like that … hundreds of them': but if imagination is at work, surely he could have done better than to recall only the 'English church', the place that looked like a castle and was not, and the 'official … bank thing with the columns up Grafton'. Fantasy would have remembered squalid dens and beer houses, not these buildings that had no relevance to the real Stephen at all. It is 'the bank thing' that comes through most clearly and most frequently. It must of course be the Bank of Ireland building, formerly the Irish Parliament House which is technically in College Green, the square from which Grafton Street runs. Perhaps it is its sheer bulk that has impressed it on whatever memory is at work as Stephen says several times 'it's big … big … bloody big', but it may be so indelibly engraved because it was at this point that he says he fell, or was knocked into the street shortly before he died.

It is with the things that concerned Stephen most personally that his ability to produce material apparently unknown to Michael is strongest and most telling. The conscious Michael has no idea where the drink that is red, white and later pink, and which gives you a mouth so terrible that you cannot swallow, sprang from. He never imagined that anyone would concoct a mixture so lethal as methylated spirits and port wine, and was astounded when he heard his voice discussing it. He was equally surprised to hear himself calling the almost-black beer 'porter': he could see and taste the drink clearly enough, and his conscious mind would have said it was

Guinness, or if pushed for another word might have mentioned 'stout'. Even when Guinness was put to him directly, he disclaimed all knowledge of it as he had done of Parnell and O'Connell, though Michael's helpless, conscious mind tried desperately to answer.

Stephen, who appeared to know so little about his world, was accurate too in the price of whiskey: when asked what a bottle of Jamiesons cost he replied without hesitation 'Whiskey? Oooo ... it's ... an *awful* lot ... (*with a tone of awe*) It's *three an' sixpence ... an awful lot*'. Michael who would have been unfamiliar with pre-decimal British currency had no idea in his conscious mind what one would have had to pay for whiskey at the turn of the century, and was staggered to hear himself quoting an accurate price.

What proved to be one of the most remarkable sequences came when Stephen was nearing the end of his miserable existence: he was living in the shell of a burnt-out building, filthy, lousy, starving and apparently reduced to the very lowest form of alcohol. Virtually all semblance of decency and humanity had gone and he was reduced to a sordid half-life. Conversation had come to a dead end but in an effort to keep some conversational link with the pitiful personality someone asked, completely at random:

Q Have you got a beard, Stephen?
A (*long pause as the character wrestled to interpret the meaning in his confused brain*) Aaaah ... a kind of a thing ... something wrong with it.
Q Why, what is wrong with it?
A Some of it's ... fallen out.

Immediately someone with medical knowledge showed keen interest and took up the questioning: Stephen's hair was similarly falling out, and when asked if he could see his skin, he held out his hands, backs towards him, feebly in front of his face. 'It's ... a kinda ... yellow ... dirty ... yellow', he replied. Extreme alcohol addiction is a very significant factor in cirrhosis of the liver which in its terminal stages often leads to jaundice (yellowing of the skin) and sometimes to loss of hair. Neither Michael, nor, one supposes, Stephen, was aware of these facts: Stephen could only report uncomprehendingly what was happening to him, and Michael was so amazed at the apparent irrelevance of the yellowing skin and falling hair that he could only suspect that his other personality had become insane.

While it is difficult, at least on the surface, to see how the American Michael O'Mara could have acquired in his present life some of the obscure material that appears in the regression to Stephen Garrett, one must remember that he has been connected with publishing for eleven years, during which time he must have read thousands of manuscripts on all subjects, fiction and non-fiction. Of these, probably the only ones that remain in his conscious memory are those that were eventually published, but his unconscious mind may well have been storing away every detail from hundreds of thousands of impossible pages. From these perhaps the young Irishman was created. In this case it would seem that under hypnosis he could equally well have become a Cherokee Indian, a French revolutionary, a Papuan headhunter, or anyone from almost any time or place. Was it pure chance that his unconscious settled on Stephen Garrett, the drunken Dubliner in the 1890s? Or was there some other significant factor which formed a nucleus round which the hidden memory could work?

Telepathy in its accepted sense seems unlikely as no one with any knowledge of Ireland was present until the last regression, and even then when much of the questioning was being done by a man who was at times almost willing the correct answers, little that was historically accurate emerged.

With Michael's Irish antecedents, however remote and diluted, it would be pleasant to attribute some of the material to ancestral memory, but as his great-grandfather left Ireland for the USA in the 1840s, half a century before Stephen's presumed existence, a direct genetic line seems impossible. Many members of the family did, however, remain in Ireland: is it possible that in some strange way beyond our comprehension the memories of some of these managed to find their way into Michael O'Mara born 3000 miles away?

Is Michael dipping into some pool of cosmic memory? If so, what has guided his mental processes to this particular character? It would be utterly incredible if from the unnumbered billions of sets of memories, random choice had selected a personality that is so completely relevant in a perverse way to Michael's own. A very similar problem arises if we consider the mediumistic approach to Stephen: why should this particular spirit leap out from the other side to speak through the body of Michael O'Mara?

One is left with a perhaps reluctant feeling that in Michael there exists some fragment of what was once part of a personality identified as Stephen Garrett. Around this core, perhaps by several other paths, have gathered the details that make the character come alive so convincingly. And this character, with its pathos and wry humour is summed up in an exchange, appropriately enough with the Irishman, that was almost the last in the series of regressions.

In this sequence Stephen had been discovered cold, wet and hungry in a derelict warehouse waiting for 'friends' – who did not turn up – with drink they had pooled their few coppers to buy.

Q If you could have anything you wanted in the world, what would you have?

A This minute?

Q Yes – this minute – other than drink, that is.

A *Well* ... I gotta think about that ... I only got the one thing?

Q Just the one thing you could have.

A Ah ... ha ... some warm clothes and shoes.

Q What about a lot of money?

A *Uh ... That's it* ... See ... I should have got that – if I got a lot of money I could get the shoes.

Q How much is a lot of money?

A (*completely ignoring the shoes and following his own thoughts*) AND THE DRINK.

5. The Jekyll-and-Hyde Theme

Sue Atkins

The following extracts, separated only by a short space of time, came from a subject who was being switched between the two main characters to which she had consistently regressed – a middle-aged Jesuit priest in the seventeenth century, who in this sequence was seriously ill, and a twelve-year-old illegitimate urchin soon after 1900, who was standing outside the village church which he had said was called St Michael's.

A (*flat, weak and unemotional*) I have no fears about the future ... God will take me ... to Him ... and that will be the beginning ... *I know* it will be the beginning ... I am not afraid. I believe in God ... I am tired of this earth ... its weariness ... the quarrelling and the fighting ... and the worldliness [Father Antony Bennet]

A (*strident with occasional obscene cackles of bravado*) You can call people bleedin'
  bastards, but if you call them bleeding Jesuses, it comes down ... that's
  what St Michael's for ... I once called somebody a bleeding Jesus ... an'
  the teacher took me out an' put my head in the school bucket ... right
  there ... an' it was winter ... an' she put it in three times ... an' then she
  said 'Spit out that word' ... and I spat it out ... *right back in the bloody
  bucket* ... [Charlie]

Both were completely sincere and consistent with the characters then speaking and it is difficult to believe that they were said by the same subject.

Even if there is no truth at all in Jung's theory of the shadow-anima,
many of us do seem to have diametrically-opposed temperaments working
inside us – the Jekyll-and-Hyde theme is not a brilliant flight of literary
imagination, but a very real and familiar human situation.

Strangely enough this division of personality which is so common in
everyday life is relatively unusual under hypnosis. Many subjects who
return to two or more 'existences' find that one of the personalities emerges
as a very positive and distinct character, while the others are so slightly
sketched in that they are little more than shadows. Others will produce
several very different lives which are described at length but which remain
cardboard stereotypes without any real individuality, rather like the figures
that stalk through a poor novel that is all plot and action. Only rarely are
two equally forceful and opposite personalities created by one subject, but
when they are they can be immensely dramatic and beg many fascinating
questions about the person's waking life.

Perhaps the most striking examples of this were the two conflicting characters produced by Sue Atkins, whose memories of her own life at five years
are given on page 11. Mrs Atkins, a professional lexicographer, who has had
very close connections with the Anglican church, regressed quickly to a
quick-witted, gutter-sharp twelve-year-old in the first decade of the
twentieth century. Charlie is the classic urchin: illiterate, living in squalor in
a farm building with his mother, the village slut, but with a brittle wit and
confidence forced on him by the continual fight to survive. Yet in spite of
his crudeness and his brashness he emerges in his short life as a warm,
vibrant and likeable character. In Sue's second regression after a short spell of
Charlie's ribald antics and backchat there came suddenly and spontaneously
Antony Charles Bennet (with one 't' he insisted), the son of a wealthy
Catholic and Royalist family in East Anglia in the mid-seventeenth century.
Brought up in the luxury of a rich wool-merchant's home and with the love
of two doting parents, Antony is the ultimate 'good boy' who conformed
in everything from dutifully learning his Latin verbs to becoming a Jesuit
priest in accordance with his parents' wishes.

Antony is, apparently, a shy, diffident, humourless but very sincere boy,
pedantically pious, but though as he develops we feel a deep respect for his
faith and his integrity, for most of his long regression he comes through as a
remote, impersonal and almost unsympathetic character. Only towards the

end does the cold façade of his dogmatic assurance crack to give us a fleeting and chilling glimpse of the despairing torments which seem to have been torturing him throughout his life. Perhaps it is just because of these agonizing doubts that for so long he projected an image of blind and unquestioning faith, as if by repeating the expected answers often enough he could convince himself that his life had not been empty and sterile.

After the first two sessions which established the characters, Sue was invariably switched under hypnosis from urchin to priest and back again several times, but never for a second did she hesitate in changing the roles instantly and completely in voice, attitude and vocabulary. And all the while Sue Atkins could only listen, sometimes amazed, sometimes frustrated, but most often trying frantically to relate what the character was saying at that moment to her own conscious experiences and attitudes. Where in the strict upbringing, the university and professional career, and the role of wife to a country parson did the coarse cackle and relished obscenity fit in? How did the pious platitudes, the grim lack of humour and the apparent blind acceptance relate to the lively and witty mind of the scholar?

The gulf between Charlie and Father Antony is clearly shown in the following extracts, though the written word cannot, of course, convey the poles between the actual quality of the voices. After an hour no name had emerged for the boy in spite of frequent attempts to get one. It had become clear that he was living with his mother in an outbuilding next to a stable by the charity of a farmer named Will. His mother, he said, called him 'Boy'.

Q She doesn't say just 'Boy' does she?
A She's dead.
Q But when she was alive, what did she call you?
A (*pertly, yet slyly*) I'm not telling you because if I told *you* what she called me you would be able to do it too.
Q Didn't she call you something nice?
A Yes. When she wanted me to go out she used to call me ... (*pause, then very reluctantly*) Chuckie.
Q Aaaah. That's nice.
A (*very sharply*). No. 'Cos it meant I had to sit outside all the night.
Q Oh, I see. What did you have to go outside for?
A Oh ... God knows.
Q Did she have men friends in?
A Well ... (*very pertly*) It didn't seem very friendly what they were doing.
Q What else did she call you besides Chuckie?
A [A sudden revelation which staggered Sue] *Charlie!*

No regression can be studied outside the context of the person making it: one must assume that the more one knows of a subject's background and history the more light is shed on the material produced under hypnosis even if, perhaps, it is only to eliminate a supernatural source of the facts. Sue Atkins speaks several languages and for the past twelve years has been the senior editor of a major English-French dictionary. In view of her exceptional command of language it seems more than mere irony that in the personality of Charlie she is completely unable to recall many simple everyday words, and in both characters the names of people and places seem so elusive that she often becomes genuinely distressed when pressed for them. Charlie especially will resort to witticisms or obscenities as he knows in some way that these will distract the questioners' attention. In this extract, which occurred very early in the regression, the name Charlie had not yet been discovered.

Q *(suddenly and quite out of context in the hope of breaking through)* What *is* your name?

A Ah ... ah.

Q What does Josiah call you?

A Uh ... oh ... *(not very convincingly)* Boy.

Q What does Billy call you?

A Well ... everything (*pauses as if looking for a way to avoid answering*) Bleeding bastard.

Q Are you?

A I'm not bleeding, anyway.

Q Are you the other?

A Well everyone is, give or take ... (*sensing the right approach and words tumble out in a rush in response to the questioner's amusement*) who knows whose father's who ... who knows who's Billy's father? Billy's got no proof Josiah's his father ... Josiah's father to half the county ...

As the church and religion naturally dominate the life of Father Antony and rather surprisingly seem to hold a strange fascination for Charlie, it is interesting to see how Sue's own background and attitudes may relate to the characters she produces. Brought up fairly strictly as a Scottish presbyterian, she became very interested in Catholicism at university, and later became confirmed in the Anglo-Catholic branch of the Church of England. Her husband, now in a lay capacity as a director of social services, was for a number of years an Anglican priest. At an intellectual level Sue now rejects much of the dogmatic and doctrinal elements of the Christian faith, but believes in the uniqueness if not the divinity of Christ, and in the reality of the mystical experiences of saints.

Is it possible that the figures of brash, blasphemous and extrovert Charlie, and the deeply religious, conformist and introvert Antony represent the extremes of her own personality inside, and that which emerges as her everyday, public image is somewhere between the two, now nearer the one, now the other, depending on the circumstances? Is she trying to resolve or justify vicariously her doubts, or perhaps to ease a hidden guilt? And once again there is the unanswerable problem – does Sue feel as she does because of experiences in her present life, or is the irreconcilable division a result of previous existences?

It was possible to explore only a few years of Charlie's short life before he died at the age of twelve, though in flashbacks he could remember a few incidents from earlier days. His story was that his mother, Ann, was Scottish (as is Sue Atkins) but when she had her illegitimate baby the long arm of John Knox stretched relentlessly over the centuries to have her driven in good melodramatic style from the family home. Of his own father he knew nothing, but on one occasion when Sue was nearer the surface than usual, he said with an irreverent chuckle, that perhaps he too was a virgin birth.

Apart from the incident with the squire's horse described on page 103 there is no mention of the years between leaving Scotland and the age of nine, when he is discovered living with his mother in the squalid conditions of a stable in a village which Charlie insists is Willingford. One wonders if the stable is in some way a symbol reflecting the strange religious/anti-religious theme that runs so strongly through Charlie's regression.

When Charlie was brought to the age of eleven Sue suddenly curled up and began to shiver violently: after a while her teeth began a very audible chatter and Charlie said he was waiting outside for his mother:

Q Didn't she say where she was going?
A She didn't tell me anything. She said she'd be back. It's dark …
Q What's the matter with your back? (*Charlie rubbed his back vigorously*)
A Cold. (*very anxiously – all his cheeky brashness gone*) I don't know why my mother's not here … she said she'd be only a little while.
Q And how long ago was that?
A That was … before milking time …

The use of 'milking time' to indicate a specific time surprised the listening Sue who had never heard it used in this context. In country districts certainly until the 1940s and probably still today, it was a standard expression to indicate approximately four o'clock in the afternoon, though the exact time varied from district to district.

It soon became evident that mother was dead – in the event killed apparently by two men who had come for her.

A They're all looking for my mother.
Q How do you know they are looking for your mother?
A 'Cos they went with torches and things.
Q What do you think happened?
A They've gone down to the river.
Q What river is this?
A The river at the bottom of the village.
Q But what is the river called?
A Aaaaaah … (*faintly*) Severn? (*more confidently*) Severn.

This was the first real clue to the area in which the episode was supposed to have taken place: although nothing has since emerged to identify the village

The Severn at Arly where there are sandstone caves. Charlie said that Josiah hid in sandstone caves near the Severn

positively, Charlie mentioned several times that the church was dedicated to St Michael, and once that a group of vagabonds with whom he took up after his mother's death were hiding in some caves. There does not appear to be a village named Willingford, but some ten kilometres north-west of Worcester there is a Wichenford, which is about seven kilometres from the river Severn, which has a church dedicated to St Michael and has caves in the sandstone rocks not far away.

The body of Charlie's mother, according to him, was found in the river battered to death and covered with blood. His reaction when the corpse was brought in 'covered with a rag' was almost word for word that of Sarah Williams (chapter 3) when her father's coffin appeared at the house.

A No ... *No (screaming) Noooo. Oh ... Oh ... (distraught) Noooooooo.* They're making me ... *Aaaaagh.*
Q They're making you what?
A Go and see her. They won't let me go ... No ... *No. (firmly and less anguished)* I don't believe that is my mother. *(very emphatically) That's ... not ... my mother.* My mother's coming back. *That's not ... my ... mother.* I won't look.

Are these really Charlie's words, or is Sue – and Ann Dowling as Sarah – really voicing quite unconsciously one of the deepest dreads in most people – the death of parents?

After this Charlie appears to have continued living at the stable, looking after himself for much of the time but during school hours at least cared for a little by the school teacher who seems to have provided him with food – often bread and cheese – at lunchtime.

Soon after his mother's death the boy appears to have attached himself to three shadowy vagabond figures, Josiah, his wife Meg, and son Billy. The four travelled round the countryside in a small cart, living rough, begging, stealing and seizing whatever opportunity offered. Charlie, who was crippled, could have been important to them to excite sympathy as they begged.

With the arrest of Josiah for sheep stealing the little group was broken up: Billy and Meg seem to have escaped, but Charlie because of his inability to run was taken to the workhouse – 'not the man's and woman's part … the part at the back'. Here, apparently a few months after his arrival, Charlie was burned to death or else so badly injured in a fire that he died of the injuries. It is interesting to note how often the workhouse theme crops up in regressions when as custodial institutions they had disappeared long before the majority of the subjects were born. Yet so savage and terrifying were the penal attitudes towards poverty of the 1834 Poor Law Act that the folk memory of the grim prisons built to house the destitute is still a powerful force, particularly in country districts. The frequency of certain themes in regressions – the workhouse and the death of parents already mentioned, the Civil War and the slums of the Industrial Revolution – makes one wonder whether folk memory does play at least a part in the apparent previous existence.

The life of Antony Charles Bennet was much less dramatic and ran its course almost inevitably as if on a track laid down for him by his family and the conventions of his society. Born at some time before 1649 ('My father says that there was a king when I was born but there is only a parliament now') he was the second son of a wealthy, Royalist, Catholic wool merchant, Richard Bennet, and was schooled on the traditional pattern of eldest-son-into-the-business-second-into-the-church.

He eventually gave the name of his home as Stapleford and when pressed for a more precise location, as there are at least nine villages of this name in England, added 'I think it is in East Anglia'. On two occasions he was specific in saying 'Suffolk'. The nearest Stapleford would be the village in Cambridgeshire, but much more interesting is the neighbouring parish of Babraham which is only fifteen kilometres from the Suffolk boundary and which contains the home of the wealthy seventeenth-century merchants, Richard and Thomas Bennet.

The Bennets bought Babraham Hall in 1631 but it was sequestred in 1651 for their support of the king. At the Restoration of Charles II in 1660 the estate was restored and Richard Bennet knighted. On one occasion Father Antony had been brought to the age of forty:

Q What is your father doing now?
A He is dead … I came home for the funeral.

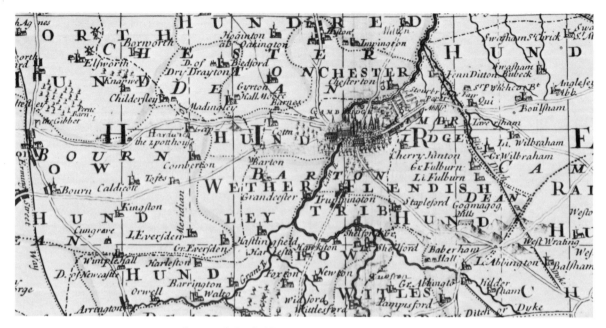

A map of Cambridgeshire drawn in 1710. 'Baberham Hall' is clearly shown south-east of Cambridge

Q What did you say his name was?
A Richard ... Master Richard Bennet ... and then he was ennobled when the king came back ... Sir Richard Bennet.

It is highly probable that the Bennets were Catholic – in secret if not in public – and there was certainly a Thomas Bennet at the head of the secret Jesuit order in the south of England in the seventeenth century. Antony said that the church in the village, which they had to attend to avoid the penalties, was named St Peter's: the parish church at Babraham is dedicated to St Peter.

At the opening of the Antony regression he was found panting and desperate, saying that he was being chased, though the reason was never fully established. He maintained that he had been questioned in a school-room by soldiers searching for his elder brother. If these characters did really exist then such an interrogation is highly likely, for the whole family, despite their wealth and position, would have been very suspect on the grounds of both politics and religion during the Commonwealth. The incident Antony referred to could well have been the sequestration proceedings of 1651.

For the rest of his childhood there are flashes of the manor house – unfortunately demolished in the nineteenth century so that the details cannot be checked – of his upbringing and his education at home. Much of the boy's conversation is artificial and precocious, but occasionally there are touches of the real child beneath the adult exterior.

At twenty-five he is in a seminary at Rome, studying to be a priest of the Society of Jesus, and fully expecting to return to England at the end of his

A seventeenth-century engraving of Poissy. Father Antony Bennet says he lived in Poissy (Puisy) after becoming a priest

training. At thirty-three he is found as a curé in the parish of Puisy-sur-Seine (or Poissy) near Paris, a little disappointed but still philosophically submissive to the inevitable.

Q Do you like France?
A I must like it if God sends it.

For the last three years of his life before what seems to be a series of strokes Father Bennet claims to have been chaplain to a 'bishop' – or at least, head of the order somewhere in the south of the country, probably Oxfordshire or Kent. It is in this period that some of the most disturbing sequences in the whole of Keeton's regressions occur: deaths one can hear in plenty – deaths by fire, by the rope, by gun and knife; deaths by disease and heart failure and the gentle sliding away of old age. But whenever Father Antony is brought to those final years he reveals most dramatically a mind in the torments of hell as doubts and regrets tear at his spirit.

As Charlie died at the age of twelve the gulf between the mature personalities of the two characters cannot be shown, but it is interesting to compare their attitudes to various aspects of life when both were boys.

Charlie gives us a glimpse of the rudimentary elementary education at the turn of the century with all the children from five to thirteen crowded in a single room with one teacher. Probably not very well trained herself, and certainly badly paid, she struggled with all ages and abilities, and to judge by Charlie she did not make much impact on illiteracy and innumeracy.

Q Can you count?
A How far do you want?
Q A hundred?
A (pause – then suddenly pathetic as his perky confidence collapses) What's a hundred?

A typical village school at the turn of the century

Q Ten?
A *You don't need a hundred.*
Q Can you count to ten?
A Oh yeh ... one, two, three, four ... five. (*long pause, then in a rush*) sixseven (*very thoughtfully*) eight (*another long pause while he whispers* 'six ... seven ... eight' *to himself*) nine ... ten.
Q Good. That's it.
A (*shouts triumphantly*) Eleven!

In one guise or another it is hard to keep religion out of Sue's regressions for long.

Q What else do they teach you?
A Counting ... writing ... Bible.
Q They teach you Bible, do they? A lot of the Bible?
A Oh yards ... it's peaceful ... it keeps them off you.
Q In what way does it keep them off you?
A If they're telling you Bible stories they don't keep saying things like 'Sit up and put your hands on your head' and 'Stop scratching, Charlie'.

Antony's schooling was very different:

Q Can you read well now?
A Mmm.
Q If I said 'amabam, amabas, amabat' could you finish it?

A *(the first real spark of enthusiasm, even if faint enough, in a dead flat delivery)*
   Amabam, amabas, amabat, amabamus, amabatis, amabant ... *(a brief pause for breath and then)* amavi, amavisti, amavit, amavimus, amavistis *(very deliberately and proudly)* Amaverunt.
Q Good – you are clever.
A I was always good at Latin. My father is going to make me a priest.
Q Your father is going to make you a priest, is he?
A *(obviously not paying any attention to the questioner, but with a face lit up with a rare flash of animation)* I *knew amaverunt* ... that is a difficult one. I *am* pleased about that ...

In contrast to the stilted tones of so many of Antony's replies which had something of a junior official reading a prepared statement, the comment on the Latin verb had all the spontaneity and delight of a child who has un-expectedly done a difficult task. The conjugation of the Latin verb produced a very interesting phenomenon. Sue was brought up on the Victorian pronunciation with 'v's sounded as 'w's and the 'i's short as in 'hit': Antony spoke them in the older fashion with the 'v' sounding as 'v' and the 'i's long as in the French *'vite'*. Sue says that her conscious mind fought to say 'amawit', but she was unable to prevent 'amaveet' from coming out.

The mild excitement of getting the Latin verb right had gone when Antony was asked his next question.

Q Do you *want* to be a priest when you grow up?
A *Oh yes* ... God speaks to you ...

No doubt father would have been delighted at such a devout reply, but he might not have been so pleased had he heard his son continue in much more enthusiastic tones:

A *And* you suddenly appear in people's houses in the middle of the night ... it's interesting.
Q And dangerous?
A *Our* priest is not frightened. *Our* priest has the same name as we have. *(as if a sudden revelation)* Our ... priest ... is ... my ... uncle ... our priest is my father's ... uncle ... Bennet.
Q So your name is Bennet [This was the first time a surname had been given]
A Mmm.

This is a significant passage: Antony had insisted that the name was spelled with two 'N's and one 'T'. Thomas Bennet (1601–1663) was the unofficial head of the Jesuit order in England about this time and travelled from house to house disguised as a shepherd to say mass. This was often done at night for reasons of safety, and made sense of a rather obscure comment earlier in the regression that the family went to St Peter's church in the village but the real service was in the middle of the night.

The broader world outside his personal problems was virtually a closed book to Charlie and the only response on current topics came quite unexpectedly when early in the regression an attempt had been made to 'date' him.

Q Who is on the throne?
A Teddy ... that's a stupid name for a king.
Q Is Teddy married?
A Uh ... (*mimes a piled-up hair style and gropes frantically for a name*) Alexandra ... silly name for a queen.
Q Have you heard of any wars recently?
A Not since Africa ... I wasn't there ... there isn't going to be another war.
Q Who said so?
A Teddy ... teacher said Teddy said so ...

How much, if any, of this is conscious memory unconsciously breaking through is difficult to say. Although Edward VII became king on the death of his mother Queen Victoria in 1901 he was not crowned until August 1902, three months after the end of the Boer War in South Africa. He did

Edward VII with his queen, Alexandra

not however acquire the epithet 'The Peacemaker' to which it seems Charlie is referring, until later in his reign. Several weeks later the subject was brought up again in the hope of clarifying some detail.

Q Do you remember when Teddy became King?
A Yes ... when his mother died ... I think she was stuffed ... we saw pictures of her and she looked as if she was stuffed ... (*long pause*) Mr Robertson in the village has got a stuffed ferret ... used to think that if you pulled the plug out the sawdust would come out ... (*pause*) maybe if you pull the plug out of anyone the sawdust will come out.
Q How long has Teddy been king?
A Not long ... he's just been crowned.
Q Did you get any presents in your village when he was crowned?
A *They* got them ... I didn't ... I wasn't on the roll.

Pressed about these Coronation gifts Charlie said, much to Sue's astonishment, that they were square tin boxes with pictures of Teddy and Alexandra in oval frames. These boxes were, in fact, very popular Coronation gifts filled either with sweets or tea.

Antony at the same age was much more aware of the political situation even if much of it seemed learned by rote and spoken in a strange flat declamatory tone:

Q Who is the king of your country?
A King died ... was killed. We've got a parliament.
Q How long ago was the king killed? How old were you?
A I don't know ... I *should* know. My father talks about it – it was before the Protector.
Q How does your father feel about Parliament?
A He does not like it. My father says that a king is a king for once and for ever ... and God made kings. And God did not make protectors.
Q Has your father said anything he does not like Parliament doing?
A (*in a strange depersonalized voice*) He says that Parliament is repressive and that Parliament orders trade, and that Parliament ... My father said that Parliament deposed kings and assumed their mantles. (*sudden change of voice from declamation to childish confidence*) My father was very pleased with that.
Q *Not* very pleased did you say?
A *Was very* pleased with that sentence.

It is in their approach to the church that the attitudes of Charlie and Antony seem, at least on the surface, to be furthest apart. Yet even here one wonders whether it is not the head and the tail of the same coin on which the inscriptions are largely irrelevant – it is still a penny or a dime whichever way it is turned, and will buy as much or as little whether it is presented with the reverse or the obverse uppermost.

Perhaps here we are coming close to the heart of the conflict inside Sue herself and her ambivalent attitude towards religion, whether this springs from her own intellectual reasoning or from some more intangible cause related to regression. Is Charlie with his irreligious backchat and his almost manic laughter at his own blasphemies being totally honest? Or is he unaware of the implications of what he is saying? Is he acting out of sheer bravado, accepting as it were the ultimate dare by flying in the face of God? His first church sequence began respectably enough, but soon deteriorated:

Q Do you know the name of the church?
A (*pause*) St Michael's. (*in a burst*) I know who St Michael was – he was the angel with the sword (*breathless with excitement*)
Q What kind of church is it?
A (*surprised at a question whose answer seemed so obvious*) Well ... it's ... just a church ... it smells inside an' it smells outside an' it's got bodies all round it.
Q What religion is it? (*it was early in the regression and a date had not yet been established*)
A Just ... a church ... got bodies all round it ... it's planted in the middle of bodies ... you gotta walk through dead bodies to get in an' then they give you pieces of somebody's dead body if you're old enough ... an' then they say (*mockingly*) I ... am ... the ... resurrection ... and ... the life. (*sudden switch to a tone of disgust*) An' it seems to me a load of b ...

Here Charlie – or perhaps Mrs Atkins – seemed to become aware of the enormity of what was being said, and the final obscenity, though obvious to all present, remained unspoken.

Antony at the same age and on the same subject was his usual detached unemotional self on the surface.

Q Do you go to church?
A Mmm.
Q Did you go last Sunday?
A Yes ... went to mass.
Q Went to mass, did you? Where?
A In our house. The priest came ... we've not to tell people.
Q No – we won't tell.
A We went to church too, though ... we go to church like everybody else, and we go to mass when the priest comes ... and the mass is real.
Q The mass is real, is it? This church you go to, where is it?
A Nearby.
Q What is the service like when you go?
A (*the only flash of feeling in this sequence*) Aaaah ... it's *boring*.
Q Is it the Protestant church?
A My mother says it's dead because they haven't the sacrament ... we wouldn't be bored if it was the real church and they had the sacrament.

Sue Atkins in front of the monument to Richard and Thomas Bennet

Because it was felt that Antony's adult life would be much more revealing than his stilted and heavily-influenced childhood, most of his regressions concentrated on the priest, Father Anthony, so that direct comparisons with Charlie are not possible. Bearing in mind that we are talking first to a sharp-witted though very limited twelve-year-old and then to a forty-year-old man who, though perhaps not academically brilliant, has had considerable experience in some aspects of life, we can perhaps profitably look at three areas they have in common.

First, both characters had a secret which they were most reluctant to reveal – Charlie's physical, Antony's mental.

In the first few minutes of Charlie's regression everything was a confused blur of running away and not running away, of hiding and not hiding, or being imprisoned in a shed whose door was wide open. Keeton seems to possess some sixth sense about such matters and guessed very quickly that the character, whoever he was for no details of any kind had been established, was keeping something back. Even later when much more of the story had emerged there always seemed something in his life round which Charlie stepped. In the second regression he was brought back to the initial hiding sequence when it was known that the vagabond Josiah had abandoned him when the gang were being chased for stealing.

Q Who are you hiding from?
A They are hiding me because they said I wouldn't go fast enough.
Q Wouldn't go fast enough ... where?
A Into the woods.

Still nothing was discovered until later in that session on a completely different subject Charlie blurted out:

A Teacher let them take me.
Q Who took you?
A Josiah.
Q Why did Josiah want you?
A (*Long pause, then embarrassed*) I ... I think it was my leg.
Q What is the matter with your leg?
A It ... it ... drags an' they ... I don' know ... he said it's a ...
Q You are a cripple, aren't you?
A Well ... I ... Uhuh ... well ... *I can walk* ...

Eventually Charlie said he had been stepped on by the squire's horse when he tried as a dare to run underneath it when it reared up. He was told to go back to the very moment when Charlie had been playing under the horse, and to bring out all the memories of exactly what had happened. In this sequence, a very remarkable one, Sue was entirely in the role of the spectator, and mentally was as much an observer as any of those sitting round the room. It was, she said later, almost as if she was listening to a radio broadcast and at the same time looking at related pictures in a book. On the only occasion when she tried, metaphorically, to turn over the page before hearing the voice she was wrong: when she heard Charlie say that he was going to run under the horse's belly, she had assumed that it would be longitudinally – out between the hind legs, that is – and was astounded when the picture showed him doing it from side to side.

This episode is one of the very rare ones in which the subject becomes quite unaware of the hypnotist or the observers, and carries on a dialogue with an invisible audience, oblivious of any questions asked.

Q Go back to the time when you were playing with the horse ... you have complete memories of that moment. What are you doing?
A Could, too.
Q Could what?
A Could too ... I'm not scared of that.
Q Not scared of what?
A Yah ... you're scared ... I'm not scared ... s'only a beast an' people are better'n beasts.

It was obvious that Charlie was not replying to any of Keeton's questions and was addressing someone that he alone could see. The dotted lines in the following sequence indicate long silences when Charlie was apparently listening to the voices of his invisible companions.

A *I could so*, Robert Williams.
....
A D'yuh *all* think I couldn't?
....
A That's got nothing to do with it.

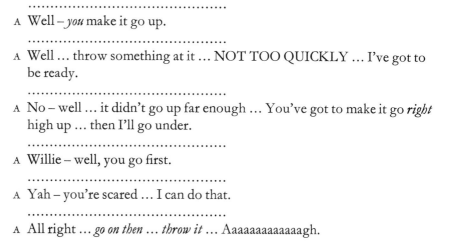

A Well – *you* make it go up.

A Well ... throw something at it ... NOT TOO QUICKLY ... I've got to be ready.

A No – well ... it didn't go up far enough ... You've got to make it go *right* high up ... then I'll go under.

A Willie – well, you go first.

A Yah – you're scared ... I can do that.

A All right ... *go on then ... throw it* ... Aaaaaaaaaaaaagh.

As the screaming broke Charlie was sent into an immediate sleep, but the personality, whatever it was, seems to have been haunted by the shame of his inadequacy for the rest of his short life.

Charlie's shame was that everyone knew that he was maimed; Antony's that he lacked the courage to admit his doubts. For an hour and a half the character that was Father Antony Charles Bennet did not swerve once from the path of the dedicated priest who in his copybook answers seemed to have subdued completely all personal human failings and weaknesses: the truth came most unexpectedly and to those listening, very disturbingly.

Father Antony, told to come to the age of forty-three, answered very faintly and wearily, saying that he had been ill for five months, that he could move nothing but his head and that his voice was now indistinct. Yet in spite of his condition he had no complaints, and only one regret – that he could no longer say mass. It was not, he added, that he could not say the words, but that he could not elevate the Host.

Q Have you any fears, father, about the future?
A Oh no.
Q What do you think will happen to you?
A God will take me ... I pray that God will take me.

It seemed that Father Antony would run true to the very last, for it seemed as if death was very near, and there was an embarrassed pause as the observers stood as it were round the invisible bed waiting for the last-drawn breath. Antony's breathing became more laboured and Keeton asked:

Q Who are *we*, Father Antony? Who are we?
A (*confidently*) Messengers.
Q Messengers from where?
A (*wearily*) I have a lot of messengers now ... especially in the nights when I cannot sleep.

The Jekyll-and-Hyde Theme

Q Where from?

A (*confidently, joyously*) God ... God. (*a sudden change of tone and a quickening of pace until the words became a confused blur*) It *must* be God ... it cannot be the Devil it must be God it cannot be the Devil it must be God ...

Q Do you have any doubts, Father?

A (*dubiously*) N ... oo.

Q Then why did you mention the Devil?

A (*frantic hysterical gabble in a very low tone*) Lord I believe help Thou mine unbelief Lord I believe help Thou mine unbelief (*the last word trailed off into a terrifying rattle in the throat as Father Bennet 'died'*)

Once the secret of the doubts was revealed Father Antony returned to it more easily on subsequent occasions, but the incident underlines yet again the problems of questioning and understanding just how the mind does work under hypnosis. Discussing the episode after the regression Sue said that as Antony Bennet she knew, even as a child who had said almost happily 'My father is going to make me a priest', there had been doubts. At the seminary in Rome (which she could recall only very hazily under

Priests bow in prayer. Father Antony wanted to enter the priesthood as a child and it was only much later that he admitted to doubts about his vocation

regression) these had been stronger and more compelling, and on every subsequent occasion the cancer was gnawing deeper and deeper into the apparently impregnable faith. She says that Antony did not talk of his agonizing uncertainty because no one asked, but one suspects that just as the real and living priest would never have admitted the tiniest crack in the blank-faced wall of his belief, neither would the re-creation of that personality by Sue Atkins, however much she had been probed. One wonders how many martyrdoms, religious and political, have been made more bitter by some festering flaw of faith that could not be revealed even at the last because of pride, humiliation or perhaps just doubts about the doubts. Was the 'My father is going to make me a priest' rather than 'I am going to be a priest' almost a cry to be allowed to reveal the truth?

The final agony of Charlie had no such mental torments; his was the sheer physical terror of death by fire. Until the very last moments when the realization of the pain dawned, he was his usual brittle, blasphemous self, jeering at the workhouse matron who had recently deloused him and who was his particular *bête noire*. He joked about how the children, of which he was the eldest, crept from the Room at night when they knew that the matron was asleep to steal a lighted coal from a fire to 'cook' stolen food. On Charlie's last night too he had obtained a glowing ember and had brought it back to the Room to cook a sparrow.

Q Where are you, boy?
A In the Room, cooking.
Q What are you cooking?
A A sparrow ... we couldn't get the feathers off properly, an' it smells ... an' she's going to smell it but we're going to eat it before she gets where it smells.
Q What kind of floor is there in the Room?
A (*nonchalantly*) Just planks.
Q Have you any beds in the Room?
A Well ... we've got ... ma ... mat ... mat ... ma ... well. Things with straw in them.
Q Doesn't the floor catch alight if you put the hot coals on it?
A (*The possibility had obviously never dawned and now that it was put to Charlie it had no real significance. It was only an abstraction he could use for another burst of exhibitionism*) No ... well ... (*pause, then a screech of laughter bordering on hysteria*) We'll ... all ... fall through ... into the basement (*screeches again*) *All of us an' a dead sparrer* (*manic laughter again, then an abrupt change of tone and attitude to apprehension*) Hey ... I ... I ... don't ...
Q What's the matter?
A (*now unusually quiet and in dead seriousness*) I didn't like what he was doing ... well ... he said he could get warm ... he said ... we could burn the window sticks ... said if we burned that we could get warm ...
Q And did he burn it?
A Theres' only one. (*genuine fear creeps into the voice – all the normal bluster of*

Charlie has gone) She's going to see the fire, y'know … 'cos it's going to show under the door. (*louder, more insistent*) She's … going … to … see … the … fire … y'know … She'll see … it. (*a long pause, then desperately resolute*) If you put the mattress on it it'll put it out … (*panic, then despairing shouts*) *Put the other one on … put … more on …* (*pause, and then the faintest whisper, far more terrifying than the screams of seconds earlier*) Bloody hell … get … out … of the way, then (*even more quietly*) Get … out … of … the way … (*screaming again*) I can't get up … I can't get up … Aaaaaaghh.

As a historian Sue Atkins in her waking state is only a little better than Charlie, but as Antony Bennet her sense of chronology once tentative dates of birth and death have been established is very good. The first positive clue to dating came when at the age of twenty-three Antony said that he was at the seminary in Rome, where he had been for two years. There was, he said, a new king in England who was foreign in his ways. Pressed further he said that he had left home while Oliver Cromwell was still alive. As Cromwell died in the autumn of 1658 and Charles II returned to London at the end of May 1660, Antony's facts could be true, and would make his date of birth 1637. This would agree with an earlier statement as a twelve-year-old that 'there was a king when I was born but there is only a Parliament now …': Charles I had ceased to have any effective rule after 1646, and was executed in 1649.

At thirty-three (that is in 1670) Father Bennet says that Charles II's sister, Henrietta, Duchess of Orleans, and a very important figure in the secret pro-Catholic Treaty of Dover between Louis of France and Charles, was dead: she did die suddenly, probably poisoned, in June 1670. Asked who was the King's minister at the time, Father Antony correctly answered 'Buckingham'.

At thirty-four (1671) he says that England is worried about the deteriorating relations with the Dutch: the Second Dutch War broke out in 1672. At thirty-seven (1674) Father Antony comments that there are very serious political problems at home, and though the 1660s and 1670s were generally very difficult, 1673 and 1674 were something of a peak. With the passing of the Test Act which excluded Catholics from public office, the ruling Cabal of five ministers had fallen, and the Duke of York, later to be James II, as well as other powerful figures, had been forced to resign from government posts. The King himself had semi-secretly become a Catholic, and under the new minister, Lord Danby, the whole emphasis of foreign relations had swung away from friendship with the French to an alliance with the Dutch. All of this news filtering through to France where Father Antony was still a parish priest, and no doubt exaggerated and coloured on its way, would be very disturbing.

In spite of some impressive historical accuracies, there were blunders: asked who most opposed the restoration of Catholic freedom in England, Father Antony replied, correctly, 'The squires in parliament …' When pressed further for specific names he said, 'Arlington … Lauderdale'. Arlington, one of the 'A's of the Cabal and himself a Catholic, was obviously wrong, and the name of Lauderdale, the ultimate political opportunist, is extremely unlikely.

There was a major historical inaccuracy when Father Antony was brought to the age of forty (1677).

Q Who is king now?
A (*hesitation*) James. [James, Charles' brother, did not become king until 1685]
Q Can you go quite freely to any town now?
A (*long pause*) It's very difficult at the moment ... you do not know the feeling of the people ... we are mistrusted.
Q Do you know who the king married?
A James? Edward Hyde's daughter.
Q But she is not a Catholic, is she?
A James is a Catholic.
Q Are there any children? Has the King any children?
A Anne Hyde has no children.
Q Anne Hyde has no children! Are you sure?
A (*silence*)
Q Perhaps you do not want to recognize them?
A James was not married to her ... her children are bastards in the eyes of God.

There is a great deal wrong in this exchange: James in 1677 was still Duke of York, but he had married Anne Hyde, a staunch Protestant. Anne had

Anti-papal feeling was very strong in seventeenth-century England

died in 1671 and two years later James married the Catholic Mary of Modena. There were two surviving children of the first marriage, Anne and Mary, both of whom became queens of England – Mary was in fact already married to William of Orange.

Although Catholic persecution is always a safe theme, it was at this period particularly violent because of the Titus Oates plot which whipped up public feeling and caused the execution of a number of innocent Catholics. Sue must have covered this period in her schooling and it does look like a confused memory of the conscious mind rather than of the unconscious. Subjects generally agree that under pressure to supply historical or other checkable material the unconscious tends often to panic and to retreat, allowing – or perhaps forcing – the conscious reluctantly to take over almost as a matter of duty. In that almost obsessive anxiety to please that is characteristic of regression, facts which are three-quarters forgotten, hopelessly confused and invented stumble out as in an examination for which not a moment's revision has been done. Under hypnosis, as in waking life, the mind produces much more significant and important material if it is allowed to go its own way rather than being forced into paths by external pressures.

It is interesting too to see how the mind can become devious and to save its own face will resort quite unconsciously to a technicality to justify what it guesses is a wrong answer. Whatever part of Sue Atkins' divided mind was in control at the time seemed to sense from the questioner's tone that a mistake had been made in the matter of Anne Hyde's children, and Father Antony, or something adopting his rigid principles for the sake of convenience, found an escape in refusing to recognize the legitimacy of a mixed marriage of Catholic and Protestant.

Of the material life of Father Antony, as opposed to the spiritual and mental, we get only a vague picture. He appears to have been at the parish of Puisy-sur-Seine (or Poissy) as one of three priests – all named Antony – at the church of St Martin or St Esprit, from the time he left the seminary until he was thirty-eight. Life appears to have been very routine, with one day scarcely distinguishable from another in the round of offices. Only occasional news of his family filtered through; elder brother Richard was killed in a skirmish shortly before the king's return; his father died and was buried in the local church: his younger brothers Philip and Robert managed the family business. All of this as well as a few pieces of more general information on the state of England and France were delivered in the flat, unemotional voice that was characteristic of most of Antony's conversation. Yet though so little of the real man hidden behind the cardboard image of the priest came through to the observers, Sue Atkins by some strange alliance of the conscious and the unconscious knew at least some of the humanity that bubbled beneath the surface.

Though he was able to suppress his own personal desires and whatever emotions he may have felt about his family, we do catch a glimpse of the gentler Antony when at the age of thirty-eight he is back in England staying, he says, with Father Bernard Reilly and Father Peter Barnaby at a house 'in the south', awaiting instructions. In this short sequence his voice was for the first time wistful and soft.

Q Do you know the name of the place?
A (*pause, then very uncertainly*) Mill? Mill? Ah, no. It's funny ... the sounds are different from a long time ago. I didn't expect it to sound like this ... Italian sounded foreign ... French sounded foreign ... and now English sounds foreign ...
Q Is it near where you were born?
A No – it's in the south. (*a sudden burst of warmth*) *The apple blossom* ...
Q Is it springtime?
A (*with immense feeling*) *Oh ... yes.*
Q Have you seen your family?
A (*curtly*) No.

And with this sharp retort almost as if ashamed of or betrayed by his inner emotions, Antony the Englishman returned from long exile becomes Antony the priest who has no family but mankind and no country but the kingdom of Heaven.

Q Are you glad to be back?
A It is God's will ... It is God's will.
Q Does that mean you would rather God had willed something else?
A (*long pause*) That does not mean anything for a priest. If God wills, God wills, and a priest obeys.
Q But don't *you* ever will anything?
A I will ... God's will. (*with a tone of complete finality*) *God's will be done.*
Q Will you wait for God's will?
A We wait for the bishop to tell us God's will. [A totally unexpected flash of Charlie – the nearest in all of his long regression that Father Antony ever came to humour.] But I suspect that God's will is a little quicker than the bishop tells us usually ...

Almost instantly the shutter of solemnity fell and as if embarrassed by the slip into near-levity Father Antony's tone became more distant and pompous again.

    This seemed to mark something of a watershed in the whole of the Antony regression: it was as if he had placed a first foot on the edge of a swamp that was to engulf him in an agony of regret, doubt and self-pity. But though he felt, as it were, the earth softening under his step and was aware of the danger, he was powerless to draw back to the firmer ground of his present comfortable if rather dull position, or even to history in general.

    As he said that he felt that he was in Kent he was asked quite casually if he knew anything of a particular nun of that county. The request was quite academic as the woman in question, Elizabeth Barton, the Maid of Kent, had been tortured and executed by Henry VIII well over a century earlier, but for some reason Father Antony was extremely upset in his replies and the body he had borrowed from Sue became very agitated physically. The sequence that followed was one of the unusual occasions on which a subject under regression argues logically completely with the attitudes and knowledge of the new personality.

A I will not think of her ... I will not think of her ... I will not think of her ... I am disturbed by the voices.

Q Whose voices are they?

A The voices of my thoughts ... my thoughts take many voices.

Q But why are you so disturbed, father?

A I am disturbed by my memories.

Q What are these memories?

A (*long thoughtful pause*) Memories of suffering ... suffering spreads ... suffering spreads.

Q Father, you know what confession is – would it not be good for you to confess?

A I have confessed. These memories have no power – they are dead memories, but they are with me. It is a sin to remember memories – memories that you have confessed and been absolved.

Q But you are remembering them, so you must be in sin.

A I *am* in sin ... because I am forced to bring back memories ... but I fear them. I fear them for what they reveal of myself.

Q But you are human, father.

A I am more than human. I am God's ... God's ... GOD's vessel.

Q I know you are God's vessel, but you are still human.

A I wish to be at peace with God ... but I am disturbed because absolution brings forgetfulness, and I have within me ... *doubts* ... and if I remember ... I am doubting God and His power of absolution.

None of the observers present was religious, at least in a doctrinal sense, but there was not a person in the room who was not profoundly moved by the very real emotions that poured out. Perhaps for some there may have been an element of embarrassment in that in the pitiless exposure of Father Antony's innermost terrors they saw mirrored some of their own.

What are we really hearing in this very dramatic episode? Are we listening to the authentic voice of a seventeenth-century Jesuit racked for some sexual indiscretion he may have committed, perhaps only in thought? Is Father Antony torn by the memory of some sin which only a completely devout man would consider to be wrong at all? Are we witnessing Sue Atkins recreating a figure through whom she is trying to resolve some hidden conflict in her unconscious mind?

After the outburst there followed a few minutes of comparative peace when the priest was brought forward six months and said that he was at the brothers' house in Kent, saying mass for them and for the Sisters of Charity nearby. The sequence was a little confused and although it was spoken in

Antony's usual flat tones, one felt all the time there was a ferment just below the surface. For one brief moment this turmoil showed itself, and then subsided again.

A When you asked me that, I thought I was in Oxford, and I heard myself answer 'The Garden', and the garden is Kent ... but the Garden of Eden is in men's hearts. (*suddenly in a very quiet aside which only the recorded tape picked up*) I am disturbed. (*normal voice again*) I am at the brothers' house, in the garden.

Father Antony said that he was still waiting to be sent to a 'parish' in Oxfordshire and as little further material of importance seemed to be emerging he was brought forward another year to see if a place name could be found. Immediately the rather high-pitched mechanical tone began and there was no mistaking the threatening tension first heard in the 'doubting' sequence behind every answer.

Q What are you doing?
A I am praying for strength.
Q Strength for what?
A Strength to live.
Q Why is it difficult to live? (*silence*) Why is it difficult to live, father?
A I have fears ... I fear the emptiness ...
Q What *are* you afraid of? (*silence*) What *are* you afraid of?
A Afraid of God's absence ... if God turns His look away from you.
Q But you have done nothing to make God turn from you.
A (*violently*) I have doubted.
Q (*gently*) Don't you think He will understand?
A (*pause, then a relapse into the dead voice*) I have led a barren life ... we must surmount the barren.
Q How do you mean 'It is barren'?
A My life of prayer is empty.
Q Why? Have you done no deeds?
A Deeds are of no account ... I have ... every priest knows from his confessional ... succour to his people ... that into one's spiritual life ... can become barren ... deserts, and a priest is God's help ... waters the desert of his people ... but there is no one to water my desert. God has turned away.
Q Why do you think that, father? (*The strange mechanical voice had become more normal, but everyone was conscious of a terrible growing horror as the words began to increase in speed.*)
A I fear God because He is not looking ... I fear God because I must live although He is not looking.
Q But why should God not look at you?
A (*extremely tense*) God ... has ... left ... me ... (*breaks down and cries in bitter fear-torn sobs*) God ... has ... left ... me ...

Q God has *not* left you.

A *God … has … left … me. (there is uncontrollable sobbing for fifteen seconds, and then hysteria. Suddenly from the depths of despair there comes an agonizing cry)* I *fear the Antichrist …*

At this point Sue had become so distraught that she had to be wakened – but this was easier in conception than execution. For over a minute Keeton's increasingly imperious commands 'Deep sleep … deep sleep, Father Antony' were ignored in a welter of frenzied sobbing, which only slowly subsided.

One of the problems in trying to explain Sue Atkins' regression is that she as herself is always searching for answers, always analysing, always doubting until doubt is no longer humanly possible. For the first two or three sessions she was reluctant to believe even that she had been hypnotized, much less regressed, and Joe Keeton was reluctantly compelled to use some of the stage techniques of post-hypnotic suggestion to convince her. After each session too she tries hard to relate the experiences of her two main characters with those of her own life – something which only she can do as she alone knows all three sets of facts, and quite naturally tends to suppress material which she feels she could not reveal publicly.

Telepathy in its usually accepted form seems to be doubtful because on the one hand the majority of the material produced by Father Antony was quite unknown by anyone present at the time, and on the other he made major errors in historical detail when the truth was familiar to at least one observer who was at all of Sue's regressions. With Charlie there was so little definite information that telepathy could have been a factor perhaps only on one occasion. In Sue's second regression which took place several weeks after the first, several people in the room were aware that the name Willingford could possibly be Wichenford in Worcestershire, and when Charlie said that men had gone to the river to look for his mother, a number of minds must have instinctively thought of the word 'Severn' – which was the answer the boy gave when asked.

Ancestral memory also seems unlikely as neither Antony, because of his profession, nor Charlie, because of his age, had children. Possibly Charlie's unknown father may have had more offspring, legitimate or otherwise, but the direct Bennet line seems to have petered out in the eighteenth century.

In the light of our present understanding, cosmic memory and spiritualism seem unlikely as a total explanation, but as all we know of these amounts to little more than total ignorance we may be trying to measure the immeasurable with our crude physical standards. However, the precise and specific nature of much of the material and the way in which Sue can leap from one character to another at different ages in rapid succession does not seem consistent with what we normally associate with orthodox spiritualist mediums. As with Michael O'Mara, the very close relationship between the characters that emerge under hypnosis and some important aspects of the subject's own waking personality are difficult to explain – we might expect a much more random selection from dipping into the universal memory or linking with the spirit world.

That Sue Atkins has some fragment of a personality that was once part of a Jesuit priest is a definite possibility. Unfortunately no Father Antony Charles Bennet can be positively identified in the Jesuit archives, but this does not entirely destroy the case as records for this period are inevitably incomplete, and almost all members of the order in England at the time had many aliases for their own safety.

Certainly the whole background – family, geography and sequence of events – is consistent and reasonable, and even if it is unusual to find a Jesuit as a parish priest, as Father Antony said he was in France, circumstances were quite exceptional in England at the time. It may have been that the officers of the order were more aware of Antony's abilities and limitations than we are, and were reluctant to allow him to return until the relationship between state and church was more fully known.

Charlie as a reincarnation is more difficult as he provides so little definite material to work on. The place was never positively identified and though as far as possible every village with a name resembling Willingford was checked, only Wichenford in Worcestershire had a church dedicated to St Michael. The workhouses in the area have no records of a fatal fire in the early years of the twentieth century, nor does *The Times* record a child dying in such circumstances anywhere in Britain about this time. It could have been that the fire was relatively minor and that the boy died perhaps weeks later from injuries, in which case it would certainly not merit a mention in the national press. As the personality of Charlie, whoever or whatever it may be, was so vague about so much, he could well be mistaken about the very basic facts of names, place and period. Further research becomes impossible, and we are forced to accept or reject his story at its face value.

There are several factors which suggest that the unconscious may be responsible for some important aspects of Sue's regression, and in particular the relationship between the two main figures she produces and her own personality is very significant. Religion has played a large part, both positively and negatively, in Sue's life, almost as a love-hate connection, with intuition and emotion on the one hand locked in continuing and unresolved struggle with reason as she sees it. The battle in her conscious mind is symbolized by the characters that emerge from her unconscious: the extrovert Charlie, blasphemous, and jeering at the church though fascinated and awed by it, and the introvert, devout but doubting and guilt-torn Antony. The frightened Charlie in the middle of a sacrilegious outburst tries desperately to convince himself that he does not believe, when really he does; the terrified Antony, at his most pious, attempts to make his reason accept every dogma of his faith, when about some he has terrible reservations.

Is it significant that the first personality to leap out of the darkness is the urchin Charlie? Is he the stronger, or is he nearer the surface of Sue's waking life? Is he the one Sue wants to get rid of, to kill off so that she can reach the deeper and more sympathetic layers of her being?

Certainly Charlie has a strong resemblance to the five-year-old Sue on her first day at school standing on the bread for the birds, at one and the same time frightened of authority yet compelled to defy it. His sharp wit, his shrewd asides, his boisterous warmth and sociability and his need to be the centre of attention are easily recognizable parts of the adult and public Sue.

As might be expected, the Antony element is less obvious as it belongs more to the private Mrs Atkins. Like the priest she is dedicated to a career to which she brings the same perfectionist ideal – though his is with faith and hers with words. In spite of her superficial confidence, the real Sue needs constant reassurance and praise – one sees flashes of the young Antony reciting the perfect tense of the Latin verb in addition to the present tense for which he had been asked, in the hope, it seems of earning some recognition. When he failed to get it he almost guiltily had to half-praise himself: 'I KNEW AMAVERUNT ... that is a difficult one ... I AM pleased about that.'

Perhaps closest of all to Antony is the deep sense of compassion with the less fortunate, and although Sue with the analytical attitude of the priest says that this springs from a sense of guilt, does it really matter what the unconscious driving force behind any action is? Does the motive or the deed count? What drove Antony to his compassion, his piety, his introspection? What drives Sue? Does the past shape the future, or does the present reflect the past?

It is interesting and perhaps revealing to see how Sue herself regards the two personalities who she looks upon with part of her conscious mind as completely detached individuals in their own right. Charlie, who springs out so readily and so quickly she finds a tiresome superficial brat with whom she has little sympathy despite his apparent warmth and gaiety. Charlie dances along on the surface of life – or would do were it not for his crippled leg. (One might wonder why, if it is the unconscious creating the character, it had to be lame.) Antony, rather colourless, ineffectual, though undoubtedly sincere, she finds a much more profound character. Although she does not feel any particular admiration or affection towards him as himself, she senses that he comes over as a cold, pedantic and rather unsympathetic personality to everyone else present. As a result she experiences a powerful instinct of warmth and protection – the very compassion that Father Antony himself showed. The gay, ebullient and social Charlie, so like the public image of Sue, she dislikes; the quiet, shy and remote Antony she finds sympathetic: does this tell us more about the personalities of the regression or about Mrs Atkins herself?

6. Benjamin Franklin's Apprentice?

Thelma Palmer

If United States citizens were given the chance to go back in person to any event in the country's history it is very likely that many of them would choose to be in Philadelphia for the Declaration of Independence or at Gettysburg for Lincoln's Dedicatory Address. This is how one American who had regressed to a character named Tom Brown claims to have remembered 4 July 1776, though unfortunately he seems to have been only a small child at the time. He was being questioned when he was an old man.

Benjamin Franklin's
Apprentice?

Q What is the most important thing you remember happening in your life, Tom?

A Independence ... Independence ...

Q Do you actually remember Independence? Do you remember it happening?

A Yeah.

Q What do you remember of Independence Day?

A I remember people shouting ... and cheering.

Q What did they actually shout?

A That Americans would be free.

Q What else happened? Do you remember any important people?

A Franklin ... and Adams ... and Jefferson.

Tom could say little more on the subject, and perhaps on the face of it a more dramatic and much fuller account could have been obtained from any schoolchild acting out the role of a witness as part of a history lesson, but they would not have actually heard the shouting, seen the moving colours of the crowd, and felt the press of the excited townsfolk as the subject did. Whatever its source, the experience of being in Philadelphia over two centuries ago was for Thelma Palmer, a fifty-year-old teacher and writer from Anacortes, Washington, as real, as personal and as vivid as if she had actually been there. When she was wakened Thelma said that she was in the middle of a street with buildings all round. She could see clearly – but

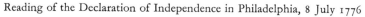

Reading of the Declaration of Independence in Philadelphia, 8 July 1776

whether she was being lifted up or whether she was fully grown she did not know.

When Joe Keeton began to work with American subjects there was considerable interest about where they might appear if they regressed to a personality in an earlier age. In England, where the population has been relatively static for many hundreds of years, not a single person has reappeared as a credible character outside the British Isles, but in the United States the whole position is very different. With a large proportion of the population of fairly recent European ancestry it was generally expected that a number would regress to personalities in the Old World – which, in the event, proved to be true. The first two American citizens to be regressed, both third or fourth generations, reappeared as personalities in the British Isles, though one of them who became a slow-witted farm girl in Devonshire, described how she had emigrated on a sailing ship in the 1850s to work as a domestic servant in Pennsylvania. Thelma Palmer, the third subject, was the first to produce a character who had been 'born' previously in the United States and, ironically enough, is easily the most recent arrival in the New World, her parents having come from Scandinavia as teenagers in the first decade of the twentieth century.

Thelma herself feels very strong ties with Europe and with European cultures, and as she watched the others telling their experiences under hypnosis she felt sure that if she could be regressed she would return to an existence on the other side of the Atlantic. So it was with utter amazement that her conscious mind, which sat helplessly throughout the session listening to what her unconscious was saying, heard her emerge as a character who could not have been more solidly entrenched in the American past had it been George Washington himself.

Her intense surprise at becoming a US citizen in the eighteenth century paled to disbelief when the very feminine Thelma heard the mind outside her twentieth-century self thinking and speaking unmistakably as a male: and disbelief turned to dismay when the new personality said that he was in Philadelphia. Her rational but speechless mind was fully aware that sitting beside her was a man who had been born and raised in that city and, to make it worse, had studied history in the university there. Thelma's only contact with the eastern side of the country is one flying visit to Washington D.C. as part of an educational programme. She has no knowledge of or interest in history, and her conscious mind, acutely embarrassed yet incapable of altering a single fact, had to listen as Tom Brown babbled of the capital as it was in the years after Independence.

The actual regression began on a timeless, non-controversial and amusing note:

Q You have full memories ... what can you see?
A (very faintly, and obviously terrified) A ... door ... door.
Q What colour is the door?
A 'Fraid to open it.

Q Why? Where does the door lead?
A Into the kitchen.
Q Into whose kitchen?
A Two ... people ... are waiting for ... me.

Slowly it came out that the character was a boy named Tom, who was sixteen years old, and though he protested that he was not really afraid, the anxiety on his face made it obvious that he was very disturbed. Although no place or date had even been hinted at, it was decided that if the secret of what lay behind the door could be resolved the other information might be obtained.

Q What is the matter then, Tom? What do you think is on the other side of that door?
A (*very tightly*) There ... are ... two ... girls.
Q Why are you afraid of two girls, Tom? Who are these two girls?
A (*again a frightened twitching grin*) One's Suzette.
Q How old is she?
A She's sixteen ... the other's Jane.
Q Why are you afraid to go into the kitchen then?
A (*embarrassed*) We ... I'm afraid they've found out ... I saw Suzette ... behind ... the barn.
Q What was Suzette doing behind the barn?
A (*very uneasy and embarrassed*) Well ... we were both there, an' ... I'm afraid Jane has found out. Jane's my *friend*.
Q What country *is* this Tom?
A (*firmly, as if talking to a fool, and a little huffy about the apparent irrelevance in the middle of his serious girlfriend problems*) The *United States* ... they have hats on [presumably the girls].
Q How many states are there?
A (*exasperated at the stupid question*) Thirteen states ...

A rough time frame of somewhere between 1776 and 1790 had been established but under regression this must always be regarded as flexible – and as was subsequently found with Tom, extremely flexible. There was some rather unproductive questioning on life and work on the farm, but at this point, early in a first regression, Thelma was obviously not happy. Her conscious mind, very much aware that with an expert on a place and period about which she knew nothing sitting beside her she was likely to make herself look silly in public, tried to intervene and rationalize. In an effort to break through this Tom was taken back to the barn incident which had apparently made a deep impression.

Q What are you doing Tom?
A (*quietly*) It's ... not ... what *I'm* doing ...
Q What is Suzette doing then?

A (*sudden change of expression – coyly*) She's putting my hands on ... her ... waist.

Q But what are you doing?

A *Well ...* (*almost apologetically*) *I'm* not doing much. (*pause, then sharply*) *Oh Suzette!*

Q What will happen if Jane finds out, Tom?

A OH ... NO ...(*panting*) We're rolling in the hay (*deep sighs of contentment*) *don't* Suzette ... don't ...

Q Don't what, Tom?

A She's ... unbuttoning ... my blouse ... *she's kissing me ...*

There was absolutely no doubt that now Thelma had abandoned her own personality, and was actually Tom in his teens. A broad outline of his life was quickly built up by moving him on in five- and ten-year steps until his death, which he said took place at the age of eighty-six.

Tom said that he had been born in a settlement called Brownsville about ten miles from Philadelphia, and there had always been an understood arrangement that he would marry Jane Seimens from the next farm. It is perhaps significant that of all the possible surnames available 'Seimens' should have emerged: Thelma knows no one of that name, which is of German origin, and Pennsylvania has one of the highest concentration of German settlers in the whole of the United States.

At the age of sixteen (according to Tom's rather erratic dating, but the context hints that it may have been a little later) he was willingly enough seduced by Suzette who subsequently drowned herself when she found herself pregnant. Although Tom's part in the paternity was in doubt as Suzette was fairly liberal with her favours, the death haunted him in a strange way for the rest of his life.

At twenty – which seems rather late – Tom says that he went to be a printer in Philadelphia because the family thought he should have a trade other than agriculture, and because elder brother Richard would eventually take over the little farm. And to whom should a printer's apprentice go in Franklin's city, but to the famous Benjamin himself.

There was a short spell when the lusty lad for a while forgot his fidelity to Jane and his romp in the hay with Suzette, and gave himself to the delights of the capital city. There are several scenes in a tavern which he says is called 'Toads' or 'Todds' and once we get a glimpse of the apprentice enjoying the commercial embraces of a Miss Lucy in a bedroom for a shilling. 'It's a lot of money' said Tom, rather embarrassed when he was caught in one regression putting his clothes on in the girl's room, 'but it is worth it because she is good at it.' At twenty-one he married Jane and returned to take over the family farm on the death of his father, Richard having been killed in the War of Independence. Here at Brownsville he spent the rest of his long life, the last fifty years as a widower as Jane had died in childbirth in her mid-thirties, leaving Tom with two daughters to raise.

It is difficult for us living in the twentieth century and completely obsessed with the passage of time to put ourselves in the past when the whole cycle of days and years was much less important. For then one week was much like the previous one, changing only in detail in the slow round of the year. There was little of the preoccupation with clocks and watches that govern almost every action we take: the date was not hurled in their faces from public buildings, TV screens and newspapers every moment of the day; their year of birth was little more than a vague entry on the flyleaf of the family Bible, and not an official statistic to be quoted on endless forms and documents. So it is not surprising that for much of his life, the eighteenth-century farm boy Tom Brown is so inprecise with dates, and we must allow him considerable latitude when he mentions a specific year.

He gives us two fixed points, which unfortunately do not agree. In one regression he says that he was fifteen or sixteen at the time of Independence and in another that he was thirty-two at the turn of the century – that is, born in either 1760 or 1768. Although after two centuries and in a lifetime which is given consistently as eighty-six years a mere eight years seems a petty quibble, the rapid sequence of events at this vital period of American history made it important to date Tom's alleged life as accurately as possible. Although there is nothing positive the general feeling of the material suggests that the later date is the more likely, and that, give or take a few years, Tom may have lived from about the late 1760s until the 1850s.

The first attempt to move Tom on beyond the affair with Suzette found him at eighteen ill with fever. There certainly were epidemics in Philadelphia all through the later part of the eighteenth century, but they were especially severe in 1779 and again in the early 1790s. In a mysterious way this fever sequence seems to link the lives of Thelma and Tom.

Q Where are you?
A (*very weak – barely audible*) Up … stairs … (*frantic gasping*)
Q Where are you, Tom?
A (*faintly*) Thirsty. (*feverishly licks lips*) Thirsty.
Q Are you ill?

Tom was then brought forward several months and appeared to be contentedly fishing on the banks of a small stream near the home farm. In reply to a question put in desperation after a long sterile sequence had brought nothing except that he had caught three trout and was happy, Tom said that he had been reading some Shakespeare – *Hamlet*. When he was asked why he had mentioned *Hamlet* and not one of the other plays, there was immediate and deep distress – so much so that Keeton suspected that Tom was still seriously ill and delirious.

Q Why, what is the matter, Tom?
A (*very afraid: voice taut and strained*) There's a … well.
Q Where is it?
A (*absolutely terrified*) Don't know.

Q What are you doing there?

A (*gasping*) Don't know. (*a frightening silence, then Thelma's face contorted with fear*) *Oh ... Oh ... Oh ...*

Q Why are you so frightened?

A I see myself (*intense distress again, then a pause, then loudly and distinctly, but petrified*) *It's not me.*

Q Who is it then?

A Don't know ... dark eyes ... *Ohhhhh.*

Q Is it a man or a woman?

A A man I think.

Q Where is he?

A In the well ... *Oh ... Oh ... Oh.*

Q What is he doing in the well?

A Looking at me.

Q Is he swimming?

A No.

Q How deep is the well?

A Twenty feet ... (*faintly, almost as if an echo from the depths of the well itself*) Twenty feet. (*suddenly hysterical*) *The moon ... The moon ... The moon ... The moon is in the well and the face is in the well ...*

Q Is the person alive?

A No ... *no* ... (*suddenly shouting*) Hamlet ... (*faintly*) I'm sick ...

The anguish was so intense at this point that Tom was brought on to the age of twenty-one when instantly he became calm, describing in flat, unemotional tones the daily routine of the little farm. Slowly, however, oblique hints emerged that the well and Suzette might be connected, though when direct questions on the girl's subsequent history were put they met obviously evasive answers: 'She's gone away I don't know where.' ' She went away with a soldier.' 'She went to Salem ...' Several times it had been indicated that Suzette had become pregnant and had been thrown from home by her parents: Tom, who maintained that he could have been responsible but that there were others who had taken her behind the barn, made up his mind to marry her, but before he could tell her, found she had drowned herself. At one point in a fairly uneventful passage discussing his life as an apprentice printer Tom became more and more abstracted as if something was preying on his mind. When he became silent altogether he was immediately put into a deep sleep and told to bring out what was worrying him. At once he became frantic:

A *The well ... The well.*

Q What about the well, Tom?

A Oh ... oh ... oh ... oh ...

Q Who *did* drown themselves in the well, Tom?

A (*the staccato 'Ohs' turned into uncontrollable and bitter sobbing. It was several minutes before the session could be continued*)

Q Tom, who *was* in the well?
A (*heart-broken sobbing with renewed frenzy*)
Q Tom, it does not matter now. It is all over. But who was it?
A S ... S ... Suzette.
Q But how did she get in the well, Tom?
A She threw herself in ... oh ... she's gone ... she's gone. (*there were alternate bouts of sobbing and cries of ' She's gone' until Tom was sent into deep unconsciousness*).

A very curious incident which seems to have some bearing on the Hamlet-Suzette-Ophelia sequence occurred in 1972, a week after the death of Thelma's father, to whom she was devoted. She received in the mail a letter which had been posted in Philadelphia, a city where, as far as she knew, she had no aquaintances. The handwriting seemed unmistakably to be that of her father, and she was extremely shocked. Inside a single sheet carried the words *'Thelma is Hamlet rearranged – a well wisher'*, which had no relevance to her life or circumstances at the time. No clue to the purport of the note or the identity of the sender has ever emerged.

Once again we are confronted, as so often in regression, with the chicken-and-egg situation: did Thelma's unconscious create the whole of the episode six years after her conscious mind had read the bizarre letter, somehow transposing or deliberately misinterpreting the meaning of 'well', or was the disturbing message some uncanny shadowing of the future – or else, perhaps, a frightening echo of the past? Or does hypnosis share with dreaming the extraordinary phenomenon of punning? Some psychologists believe that the mind in sleep will play with words – especially homophones – perhaps because it feels that unpleasant situations can be made more acceptable if they are presented, as it were, in disguise. For example, a person who is dreading having to make a sea voyage because he is invariably sea sick may have a terrifying nightmare of being blind. Although there seems to be little connection between his fears of the journey and loss of sight, the mind may twist 'sea' into 'see' and then into the horror of 'not-seeing'.

Whatever the reason behind the strange Hamlet-well sequence, it was only a fascinating detour from the main historical regression, the real heart of which lies in the years about 1780 to 1790 when Tom says that he was living in Philadelphia apprenticed to the printing trade. The family farm seems to have been a fairly humble affair, perhaps little more than a subsistence holding for on several occasions he says they have few cows, some chickens, some fruit trees, and grow corn, pumpkins and vegetables. In his later life Tom says that he does take a few things such as vegetables and fruit to market in the city for cash, but on the whole it seems a very close to the earth existence. If we are listening to real memory then anything different from the comfortable but routine round of work on the land must stand out as a sharp highlight in a very ordinary life, and Tom's short stay in the capital was easily the greatest event of his eighty-odd years. If anything could persist, it would surely be those days in the great city. It is during this period too that the only really verifiable material is produced, and it must be emphasized again that the conscious Thelma knows absolutely nothing of the city or its people.

Having picked up the farm boy in the first session and having established where he lived, it was fully expected that this would be just another of the unmemorable accounts of rural life that seem to form ninety per cent of all regressions. So when Tom was brought forward from sixteen to twenty-five and said that he was on the farm it was assumed that he had spent the whole of the intervening years there caring for cows and picking pumpkins. But the next exchange caused a flurry of interest.

Q Have you lived on the farm all your life?
A I lived in Philadelphia once.

Benjamin Franklin with the *Pennsylvania Gazette* lying at his feet

Q What were you doing in Philadelphia?
A I was an apprentice.
Q What were you learning?
A Printing ... printing.
Q Who was teaching you?
A Ben.
Q Who?
A Ben ... (*long pause*) ... Franklin.
Q What sort of things did he print?
A He printed ... calendars ... and almanacs ...
Q Any newspapers?
A The ... Uh ... *Gazette*. I didn't work on the papers much.

Exciting and full of potential as this opening was, it underlined at once the problem of dates and times that run throughout Thelma's regression. Benjamin Franklin died in 1790 at the age of eighty-four and had given up active participation in the printing business in Philadelphia about 1748, though it did continue to run under his name until 1765. He did however maintain a strong interest in the trade until the end of his life, setting up private presses elsewhere in America and in Paris when he was there. The *Pennsylvania Gazette* which he personally published from 1727 until 1748 did continue to have links with the old man and his ideas right until after his death. But Franklin would certainly not have had anything to do with a humble apprentice in the second half of the century – and in any case, he was living in Paris from 1776 until 1785. It may or may not be relevant, but in France, Benjamin became interested in hypnotism and attended sessions under the famous Franz Anton Mesmer himself. Though the dating looked like the end of the road for any credibility in Tom Brown as Franklin's apprentice, perhaps he should not be dismissed as lightly in the strange context of regression, and there are several possible explanations for the discrepancies. If these are memories of actual experiences then there may be the telescoping of two distinct personalities – perhaps one who lived earlier in the century and who was genuinely an apprentice of Franklin, and one who lived later and who was a farmer. It may be that Tom Brown is consistently twenty to thirty years out in his reckoning, and it has been noted frequently in Keeton's regressions that the further away the existence the more likely the chances of confusion over time. Or perhaps the fame of Benjamin was so great that every apprentice who worked in the city as long as he was alive claimed to have been serving under the master himself.
   Obviously the next step was for Keeton to take Tom back.

Q Go back to the time when you were printing with Ben Franklin. What are you doing?
A Taking letters up ... putting them up. [The use of the phrase 'putting them up' is interesting as it is a very old technical expression used by compositors and would not normally be used by anyone outside the trade.]

Benjamin Franklin visits a printing shop where an apprentice puts up type in the background, just as Tom Brown would have done

Q Setting up type are you? What are you printing?
A One sheet ...
Q What does it say?
A (*pause – subject leaned forward slightly and appeared to be concentrating on reading something in front of her*) I can't read it.

This was obviously not because Tom was illiterate but because the words would not come clearly to his inward vision: in a later session he managed to decipher part of the notice he was setting as '*Installing ... a ... bell ... Liberty Bell ...*' The Liberty Bell, brought from London about the middle of the century, had heralded the Declaration of Independence and was re-hung in 1778.

Q Who is with you?
A Ben is in the back.
Q Is Ben married?
A It's hard ... to say (*pause*) *I don't know* ... I don't know. (*long pause and a look of intense concentration*) There are *two* women ... and they won't go together ... I don't know ...

On being wakened up Thelma said that she had had a strange experience: she had always assumed that Ben's marriage had been regular enough, but that as Tom she had seen two female figures separated by a tall column or pillar, and try as she might to get them to fuse into a Mrs Franklin, they refused to merge. Neither she nor anyone else present was aware of the complex situation surrounding Franklin's matrimonial arrangements.

Before leaving for Europe Franklin had become engaged to Deborah Read, the daughter of his landlord, but she, perhaps a little impatient, married a ne'er-do-well potter, John Rogers, in the summer of 1725 while her fiancé was abroad. It is not clear whether Rogers was in fact free to marry at the time as there was suspicion of a previous wife. If there was, or if she was dead or alive, no one was certain, but as it happened it did not matter much as Rogers deserted Deborah after a few months and vanished to the West Indies to escape from creditors. Franklin returned to America in 1730 and promptly 'married' Debby without any official or religious cere-mony. But the legal position is still unclear: was Rogers still alive? Had he ever really been Deborah Read's husband? Was there an earlier wife, and was she still alive? Who, if anyone, had committed bigamy, and with whom?

An additional factor in Tom's confusion over the identity of Mrs Franklin may have been Ben's amatory adventures both before and after his 'marriage' to Deborah, who died in 1774. Tom certainly seemed to be aware of this aspect of Benjamin.

Q Does Ben print any newspapers?
A (*very forcefully, as if to a fool*) Yes – The Gazette.
Q What else does he print?
A Almanacs ... Poor Richard's ... Poor Richard's Almanac.
Q What else is Ben interested in? Just books and newspapers?
A (*loud derisive laughter*)
Q Why, what are you laughing at, Tom?
A Ben says 'Fish and company stink in three days.'
Q But is he interested in anything else?
A Ben's ... interested in everything ... kites ... and stoves ... and *ladies*.

The 'fish and company' saying is first quoted in John Ray's *Compleat Collection of English Proverbs* (1670) but was quoted in the 1736 edition of *Poor Richard's Almanac*: in her conscious life Thelma had never heard of it.

Ben's family affairs were returned to in a later session.

Q Does Ben have any children, Tom?
A (*a change of expression to a sly grin, almost a leer, and then a forceful*) Nooooooo.
Q Why do you say it like that?
A Ah ... ha ... (*chuckles to himself*)
Q Perhaps he is not married, and that is why he has no children?
A Ah ... ha ... (*chuckles more loudly*)

Tom was wrong in saying that Benjamin Franklin had no children, but his negative was not really a negative at all. There was a son (who died in infancy) and a daughter by Deborah, as well as at least two other children by different women, but whether even Deborah's were technically legitimate in view of the strange circumstances surrounding the marriage it is impossible to say.

Tom was extremely vague on the process of printing, and could say no more than most people know, apart from the one strangely appropriate expression in referring to setting, 'putting them up'. He could not name any of Franklin's other employees, nor any rival printers in the city: in fact, the only other piece of information directly relating to Franklin came un-expectedly in the middle of a completely different topic – 'Ben lives in the High Street …' Simple though this comment is, it is significant for the Franklin properties were all on Market Street, which had been earlier called High Street, and on some late-eighteenth-century maps was still marked 'Market (or High) Street'.

Apart from this one important point Tom is vague on the topography and architecture of the city: Independence Hall is mentioned several times but he cannot name its exact location. Of the churches he will admit only to the Quakers Meeting House, which even the dullest student could guess was relevant in Philadelphia, but he is more forthcoming on the library which seems to have meant a great deal to him. On three occasions he is found there, reading, or writing poetry with a quill pen.

Q Is there anything outstanding about it? [i.e. the library] What is it made of?
A I like the room where I sit the best … the floor is hard … stone.

Library and Surgeons Hall in Philadelphia, 1779

Benjamin Franklin's
Apprentice?

Q But from the outside, is the building of wood?
A No … stone.
Q What colour?
A Grey.
Q Has it a flat roof?
A Pointed … pointed … pointed.
Q Who started this library?
A (*suddenly alive*) *Oh that man … that man …* (*struggles to recall a name*) J … J … J … um Jefferson? … *no.*
Q Is he a rich man?
A Yes.
Q Is it Jefferson?
A *No.*

As so often with Tom there are so many near-misses – little pieces of information that could be sheer chance, or else highly significant. Libraries flourished in Philadelphia at this time – the Junta Club formed by Franklin in 1728 grew into the Library Company of Phildelphia in 1731, and this in turn was absorbed into the Union Library of 1769. Shortly before he left Philadelphia, which if the later date of birth is accepted could have been 1794–5, Tom was found in the library once more, saying that he was reading poetry.

Q Who writes the poetry you like best?
A (*instantly*) Wordsworth. (*long silence*)
Q Who else do you like?
A (*more hesitantly*) Spenser.

Thelma, who is very much a contemporary poet was astonished as Wordsworth was little more than a vague name from college days and Spenser even more remote. Her waking mind, listening helplessly, was furious at the ignorant Tom blurting out the name Wordsworth because though she knew so little about him she was certain that he had not been writing as early as 1794 – a view shared by almost everyone in the room. When the point was checked however because the first words Thelma spoke on being wakened were 'I'm sorry about that mistake with Wordsworth, but Tom insisted …' it was found that his two books, *An Evening Walk* and *Descriptive Sketches,* were published in 1793 and 1794 respectively.

Apart from Independence Hall and the Library the only locations that occur in Tom's regressions regularly are State Street and a tavern called Toads or Todds. Typical of the context in which these occur are the following:

Q What did you say the name of the street was?
A State Street. *State Street* (*angrily*) *I told you before.*
Q Why do they call it State Street?

State House, Philadelphia, 1778. Tom can remember this impressive building long after he has returned to the farm

A *The buildings.* The government buildings ... I go there quite often.
Q Do you go into any inns?
A Yeah ... I have ale ... and ... mmm cider.
Q Where?
A Down at The Toad. (*silence but three deep sniffs in succession – Tom chuckles to himself and says that he is taking snuff*)
Q The Toad, Tom – is that the correct name of the place or is it the nickname – the name that's given to it?
A That's what all of us call it – The Toad.
Q Who runs The Toad, Tom?
A A woman.
Q A woman, is it? What is her name?
A Sally.

Certainly a repulsive name like The Toad seems out of place among the traditional Black Swans, Seven Stars, Three Tuns and Rose and Crowns that operated in eighteenth-century Philadelphia, but there are two possibilities which might account for it: it could be a nickname based on a badly drawn signboard or some trivial and forgotten incident which took place there, or it could be a misinterpretation of a surname. Robert Morton's diary (1777) records that he visited a Mrs Toys Tavern in Upper Reading Road in Philadelphia, and the name Todd was very well known in the city. Benjamin Franklin's postal records show that there was a Todd's Ordinary (a tavern eating-house) at Finchville as a depot for the mail, but this is too far away for the most optimistic of Tom's off-duty junketings. Nevertheless, the possibility of a hostelry which Tom knew as Toads cannot be ruled out.

There is no record of Chestnut Street where the State House was situated ever being called State Street, but there was a State House Yard where many of the government offices were situated in the late-eighteenth century, and on some late nineteenth-century maps there is a State Street.

On one occasion Tom was asked about theatres, but at first seemed very uncertain: he suggested that plays might be acted in some of the taverns – which would be well in the tradition – and also that there might be a small theatre with a name: '... something about lights ... Suh ... Suh ...' and then gave up perplexed because he could not remember. Theatrical performances were officially illegal in strict Pennsylvania, but some were put on in Philadelphia though whether with amateur or professional actors is not known. The Old Southwark (pronounced Suthark) Theatre was built in 1776, but not declared legally open until 1789, even though George Washington had watched a performance there earlier. Is it possible that this is the name 'Suh ... Suh' for which Tom's memory was groping?

An intriguing and important exchange took place when questioning – or rather, answering – had petered out into long silences, and in an effort to find a new track that would stimulate Tom's memory, the subject of money was brought up.

Q Do you have any money?
A Yeah. I have some coins in my pocket.
Q Have you a dollar?
A (*silence*)
Q What is the smallest coin you have?
A (*the exasperated talking-to-an-idiot tone*) A penny of course.
Q And the largest?
A A shilling.
Q How much are you paid?
A Two shillings a week.

The dollar was not adopted as the unit of currency until 1787 up to which time the terms pounds, shillings and pence were used, even if the Spanish and other foreign coins that were in wide circulation had to be converted into them. There is no doubt too that the older British nomenclature persisted for many years after the changeover, so that Tom was quite consistent.

On the very last occasion in this series of regressions that Tom was taken to Philadelphia he was in the library once more.

Q Do you read the newspapers?
A Some.
Q What sort of news has been in the newspapers lately?
A Um ... Government news ... people.
Q What news has there been about the government?
A New laws ... something about money. [This sequence was weeks after the previous one]

Q What about money? The amount? The names of the money?
A About the making of money.

There were three important pieces of monetary legislation about the time: the dollar was, as we saw above, made the official unit in 1787; a mint was set up in Philadelphia in 1791; and the following year an act enforced a standard currency system in all of the states instead of allowing each to decide on its own.

With the end of the Philadelphia sequences most of the verifiable material ceases, but the remaining years add much to the personality of Tom. When he was about twenty-one he married Jane and a few years later he returned to Brownsville to run the family farm when his father died. His elder brother Richard, he said, had been killed in the War of Independence: in this brief extract Tom gives vent to the only bitterness and hatred he utters in his many hours of regression. This is more surprising as the conscious Thelma is very pro-British.

Q Why do you have to go back to the farm, Tom? Is there no one else who can manage it?
A (*slowly, emphatically*) My ... brother ... is ... dead. (*viciously*) Dead.
Q How did he die, Tom?
A (*savagely*) In the war.
Q Who were you fighting, Tom?
A (*no reply, but deep unhappy gasping*)
Q Who *were* you fighting, Tom?
A (*vicious again*) They've gone now. I don't want to talk about it.
Q But we would like to know who you are fighting.
A (*shouting very loudly – voice full of hatred*) The British.
Q Where was he killed, Tom?
A (*long pause, then sobbing*) Potomac ... in the winter ... in the winter.
Q How long ago was that, Tom?
A I don't know ... eight ... ten ... years perhaps ... I don't know. (*suddenly shouting again, full of fury*) The damned British ... the damned British (*breaks down*)

There were many skirmishes all up and down the Potomac during the War of Independence and as some of the younger British officers were trying to adopt the highly successful guerrilla tactics of the Americans, casualties tended to be high in relation to the number of men involved.

For the remaining half century there is little but the quiet life of the little farm and the growing family, with much of the material that does appear in the form of flashbacks from the ageing Tom. There were, he said, two surviving daughters, Susan and Jenny, and though there had been other children they had all died in infancy, which is quite in accordance with the terrible mortality of the period – perhaps in the best circumstances one baby in three died, and with Tom's family, circumstances were not good. Jane herself died in her mid-thirties, again a classic picture of the rural wife, worn out with work on the farm and in the house and with constant pregnancies an easy prey as her youthful resistance to disease began to falter.

At the death of Jane there were no words – only bitter tears and grief so agonizing that Keeton quickly moved Tom on to another age.

As happens from time to time in Thelma's regressions just as one has reached a point at which there seems nothing more of any value to be unearthed and that further dialogue is so vague that it could easily spring from imagination, there comes a word or phrase or face that makes the whole thing significant again. So it was that Tom had been taken to the age of thirty-five and was found at a Thanksgiving party. Throughout this fairly long sequence Tom was standing on one leg in the corner of the room – why, he did not know. He said that it was not a game, and that he did not think he was injured – he just had no explanation, and if it was some punning reference, the truth was never discovered, unless it was an oblique way of expressing his loss in Jane's death. Although it was six weeks since the regression in which he had described his wife's death, in this one he mentioned immediately that she had 'been gone nearly a year now'. After some desultory conversation he said that he had had 'turkeybird and hard cider'.

When the word 'turkeybird' was discussed later with Thelma, she said that she had never consciously heard it: her rational mind knew that Tom was trying to make her voice say 'turkey-BIRD' and as it sounded so ridiculous she had tried to stop after the first word, but could not. The expression seems to be obsolete now, but it was common in the eighteenth and nineteenth centuries.

In the last session Tom was found at an unspecified age but apparently elderly for his voice was rather querulous. As he showed signs of distress he was asked if he was ill.

A No ... I feel ashamed.
Q Why are you feeling ashamed?
A There's a black man working on the farm.
Q But why are you ashamed there is a black man working on the farm?
A I don't think he should be working like that.
Q Why not?
A He's human.
Q Do you pay him?
A No ... I ... he lives here.
Q Why do you feel badly about this one?
A He's old.
Q Is he badly treated?
A Not by me ... the other men.

It is interesting that Tom said that he had not bought the black man, and later was emphatic that his father had not either, so that it was obvious that he was not talking about a slave, even though the listening Thelma thought he was. When Thelma was wakened she was asked when slavery had been abolished in Pennsylvania and replied that she supposed it was after the Civil War (1865). Actually Pennsylvania had outlawed the practice in the late eighteenth century so that once again Tom had given the correct answer against her natural inclination.

Finally, Tom was brought to his last memories: instantly his body slumped and became limp and feeble. The breathing was laboured, and when asked if he was in pain his hand, trembling and apparently with great effort, wearily touched his chest. He said that his youngest daughter, Jenny, who was then 'in her sixties' was with him, but no one else. For a few seconds his breath grew harsher, then faded until it was scarcely perceptible: then it stopped altogether and Tom's head dropped to one side. An old, old man had slipped away peacefully and naturally – but where had the real essence that had been Tom gone?

How does one sum up the regression? Two weaknesses seem to stand out if we consider it as an historical experience: the imprecise dating of the Franklin/Philadelphia sequences, and the omission of many of the shattering national events that were taking place at the time. Even if Tom was not interested in the wider political issues one would have thought that important local events such as the occupation of the city by the British in 1777–8 would have left some memory. It could be, of course, that the right questions were not asked all through: with Tom especially it was obvious that the answer being sought often came from a reply to the most unlikely question when all the apparently direct approaches had brought nothing.

Perhaps too we are looking at the whole picture with different eyes, and then with hindsight. We see events from two hundred years later distilled from documents and statistics, and judged in the light of their long-term results. We do not know how the people felt at the time, perhaps uncomprehending, perhaps apathetic, perhaps not interested as long as pumpkins grew and cattle bred. If Benjamin Franklin in millions of words can project only a tiny fragment of the real personality through which he perceived the world and times, then what can we expect from the anonymous and incoherent Tom Browns and Jane Seimens?

On the other hand there are strengths in the regressions: the period accuracy is consistent with only a few anachronisms – and these generally occur towards the end of a long session when the subject is tired and for the moment the rational mind of Thelma tries to impose an answer on Tom. There is a steady stream of material – words, expressions, place and personal names, situations and atmosphere – which are correct and which are quite outside Thelma's conscious store of knowledge. It is not so much as if she is sending a few brilliant and unexpected shots into the bullseye, but building up a formidable score – and case – by sinking dozens of shots into the outers.

All interpretations of regression must, of course, be subjective, but Mrs Palmer's story seems to follow the general pattern. In trying to find the most acceptable explanation one can perhaps eliminate genetic memory: Thelma's ancestry is pure Scandinavian so that any direct lineal descent from Tom Brown seems beyond the bounds of possibility. Telepathy as we know it must also be doubtful because when the questioner from Philadelphia was present and almost willing the answers from Tom, little material on the city or its history emerged – indeed, if anything his presence seemed to have an inhibiting effect, and most of the information came when there was no one in the room who had any knowledge of the place or time.

The principle of universal knowledge has some appeal despite the problems of understanding the whole concept and its mechanisms. The idea of Thelma-Tom groping half-blindly in some psychic store of material relevant to the place and time could offer an explanation for the inconsistency and confusion of dates and characters, but why so much extremely trivial material should be accessible, or even stored at all, when more important details are either absent or unavailable is extremely puzzling.

We are compelled once more to look at the poles of explanation – genuine reincarnation, some function of the unconscious mind or, perhaps, a combination of both. Does Thelma Palmer possess some essence which was once part of a Tom Brown which bears with it not only personality traits but also fragments of physical memories? If so, what happened to that element in the seventy years between the death of Tom and the birth of Thelma? Has there been another existence between the two in which this same element inhabited another body – the time interval looks about right? Are the inaccuracies caused by the experience of one or more lives mingling with that of Tom, or is that merely because memory in some incorporeal world fades and confuses as it does in the physical one? Whatever the answers to these questions the inexplicable possession by Thelma's unconscious of some highly obscure and specific pieces of information which could have been available to Tom Brown does seem to indicate a link between the two minds.

Or are there two minds? Is the story an uncontrollable outpouring of the unreachable depths of Thelma's mind? One can certainly read some of the twentieth-century woman's character and attitude in the eighteenth-century man, and there is that strange incident of Hamlet, which seems to spring from the present. But it is always the factual knowledge that presents the difficulty, and this is at the core of Tom's regression: are we looking at Thelma-Tom or Tom-Thelma?

7. Read or Remembered?

Edna Greenan

Q Where are you?
A (*dead silence, but a frantic licking of the lips*)
Q You have complete memories. Where are you?
A (*more licking of the lips which had visibly become dry*)
Q Where are you?
A On a stage.
Q What are you doing?
A Hast got a drink?

With this rather inauspicious exchange that seemed to indicate another routine and relatively ordinary figure stepping out of the past began one of

Joe Keeton's most enigmatic regressions. For over eighty hours Edna Greenan, a fifty-seven-year-old Liverpool housewife, who had not come originally as a subject but had somehow slipped into the role, has consistently assumed the character of the actress and courtesan Nell Gwynn (1650–1687).

Edna left school at the minimum age – then fourteen – and worked in a number of factories and shops, and at the same time bringing up a family of five children. Even at her most sanguine, Edna would deny any pretension to, or even interest in, literature or history, and though she was aware of the name Nell Gwynn before her regressions, she knew virtually nothing of the person nor of the social and political background.

In theory of course, all of the biographies of Nell, from the earliest in 1750 to the most recent, as well as the whole of Pepys' 'Diary' and scores of documents in universities and libraries are open to Edna, but she would be the first to admit that she has neither the scholarship nor the time to study them. She categorically states that she has never looked at any book on the subject, and to remove any doubts on the matter, Keeton put her under deep hypnosis as herself.

Q You are Edna ... you are Edna in 1978. I want you to go back to the time when you were reading a book called 'Nell Gwynn' by Bryan Bevan ... a book about Nell Gwynn written by Bryan Bevan.
A (*deep frown ... head turns from side to side in bewilderment*) Eh ...?
Q I want you to go to the time when you read ANY book about *Nell Gwynn* ...
A (*same puzzlement ... shakes head*)

The same technique was repeated for films, TV plays and the theatre, but all brought the same puzzled negative response, and eventually a definite denial. Keeton is sure that she would have been quite incapable of lying under the circumstances. Even if Edna had learned the most comprehensive work on Nell Gwynn by heart it would not have been much use because perhaps the most amazing aspect of this case is the unerring accuracy with which she assumes the complete character at any specific date to which she is sent. In a single two-hour session she may be switched to half a dozen different periods of Nell's life – from five to thirty-seven, and then back to ten, twenty-two, sixteen and twenty-eight. Instantly the mood changes appropriate to the date, and at each stage only the memories that the historical Nell would have had begin to pour out. One may understand this in a computer, but not in a human mind.

Analysing this vast amount of material is a formidable task. The majority of Edna's answers fall into five categories: those which are known to be historically correct; those which are definitely known to be incorrect; those which seem to be near-misses, half truths or fortunate guesses; those which seem to be small talk, or imagination; and those which on the face of it present completely new historical material. If only we could be sure that these last pieces of information were accurate and not just imagination, they would be absolutely invaluable. Unfortunately, in view of the known inaccuracies they must always be classed as 'possible' or 'unproven'.

The next four short sequences show some of the problems of trying to make objective judgements on Edna's regressions. In the first she had been taken to 1673 when the original Nell Gwynn had been Charles II's mistress for four years, had borne him two sons, and was comfortably installed with her mother in a smart house at 79 Pall Mall, London, only a few hundred metres from Whitehall Palace.

Q Do you do any acting now?
A *No* ... no, not now.
Q Have you ever been in plays?
A Yes, I've been in lots.
Q Which ones in particular?
A Oh – I'll tell you one I'd a liked to be in but I never got to be in it. They said I weren't good enough. 'The Tempest' by Will ... i ... am Shakespeare.
Q What part did you want in that?
A Miranda.
Q What other plays have you been in?
A I've been in 'The Maiden Queen'.
Q Who wrote that?
A Dryden.
Q And what part did you have in that one?
A I were a mad woman.
Q Who was in it with you?
A Charles Hart. He taught me all I know about acting.

Nell was correct when she said that she was no longer on the stage as her acting career ended in 1669 when she became the King's mistress. One of her greatest triumphs was the demented Florimel in Dryden's 'Secret Love' or 'The Maiden Queen' in which she played opposite Charles Hart as Celadon. It was indeed Hart who introduced her to the stage and taught her the craft of acting as well as becoming her lover. Edna-Nell's quirk of referring to plays by their subtitles and actually refusing to acknowledge the main title when it is put to her is very strange and will be discussed later when her acting career is dealt with in more detail. Nell Gwynn never did act in 'The Tempest' but it is known that the play fascinated her and that she watched it four times in six weeks. But it was not her ability alone that prevented her acting the part of Miranda, for 'The Tempest' was on the repertory of the Duke of York's Company, and by an arrangement between the managers could not be played by the King's Company, of which Nell was a member. Nell comes back to this play several times during the regressions and on one occasion which will be described later gives some unknown details of the production, which would be extremely valuable to theatrical historians, if only they could be relied on.

Q Did you do any other parts?

A I were in Eighty Eight Days ... or Eighty Eight Years ... I've forgot.

Q Who wrote that one?

A Not right sure now. Don't know whether it were Dryden, or Killigrew ... or now who's that other one? Oh ... Bucks ... he tried to write something.

The title page of the play *Secret Love* by John Dryden which Edna insisted was called by its subtitle *Maiden-Queen*

SECRET-
LOVE,
OR THE
Maiden-Queen:

As it is Acted

By His Majesties Servants,

AT THE

THEATER-ROYAL.

Written by

JOHN DRYDEN Esq;

―――――*Vitiis nemo sine nascitur ; optimus ille*
Qui minimis urgetur.   HORACE.

LONDON,

Printed for *Henry Herringman*, at the Sign of the *Anchor*, on the Lower-walk of the New-*Exchange*, 1668.

Q Who is Bucks?
A Er ... Buckingham ... Er ... I'm thinking of some more. I used to do a lot of talking. I'd talk before and I'd talk after.

Nell Gwynn appears to have acted in a little-known play called 'Queen Elizabeth's Tragedy', or 'The History of Eighty Eight' by Thomas Haywood, and there may be some confusion with another contemporary play 'Adventure of Five Hours'. This is the second occasion on which Nell emphatically gives the subtitle rather than the better-known name.

As well as the 'mad' parts for which Pepys praised her so highly, Nell was also famous for declaiming the obligatory prologue and epilogue – the 'talk before and the talk after' to which she referred. Even in high tragedy the epilogue was usually bawdy, satirical, political or full of double entendres: in 'Tyrannic Love', for example, in which the real Nell played most inappropriately the virtuous Valeria who in the last act died of love, she leaped from the bier as it was being carried off at the end of the play and ranted her epilogue which ended:

> O Poet, damn'd dull poet, who could prove
> So senseless as to make poor Nelly die for love.
> Nay – what's worse, to kill me in the prime,
> Of Easter term, in tart and cheesecake time ...

The meanings of 'tart' and 'cheesecake' do not seem to have changed much over the centuries. Edna-Nell made several oblique references to this famous epilogue, but could not quote any lines from it, however hard pressed.

Q What is the queen's name?
A (instantly) Anne-Marie.
Q Where does she come from?
A Port ... u ... gal.
Q Can she speak English?
A Not very well. She can say one or two words, but she's better now.
Q Has she got any children?
A No.
Q Why not?
A How the bleedin' hell should I know?
Q I'm sure you ought to know.
A Well ... Charlie's wearin' hisself out with everybody else. If he'd stop with her a bit more he might have some with her.
Q So you have got all her babies?
A Looks like it. But she likes Mortimer.
Q Who's Mortimer?
A Lucy Walter's bastard.
Q Is he really called Mortimer?
A I think so. I call him Mortimer. Laurence calls him Mortimer.

This short extract from a longer sequence gives examples of four of Edna-Nell's categories. It is true that Charles' Portuguese wife, Catherine of Braganza, had no children and this led to considerable consternation as the King's brother James, Duke of York and a known Catholic, was heir to the throne. In spite of what must have been intense unhappiness and humiliation at seeing her husband's ever-growing number of 'royal bastards' Catherine always showed, as Nell says, great kindness towards Charles' illegitimate son by Lucy Walters, the handsome, weak and unpleasant Duke of Monmouth. Edna-Nell commits the incomprehensible error of calling the queen Anne-Marie, both here and throughout the regressions. If Edna were even unconsciously remembering from a biography she would hardly be likely to make such a blatant error, and yet she is consistently wrong. The only possible explanation other than a straightforward mistake is that it might have been a pet-name for the Queen, of whom Charles, despite all his infidelities, seemed to have been very fond. Why, too, one wonders should Edna-Nell consistently refer to Monmouth as Mortimer?

The remainder of the extract could be no more than chitchat or repartee that Edna might indulge in her present life; the use of 'bleedin'' – which Edna-Nell does frequently – is very consistent with the real Nell Gwynn of whom Pepys says after visiting her in the green room ... 'how lewdly they talk ... to see how Nelly cursed ... was strange'.

The sequence continued:

Q Who is Laurence?
A Laurence Hyde.
Q Who's he?
A Mr Hyde's son.
Q I can guess that. What does he do?
A Who? Mr Hyde or Laurence?
Q Either.
A Well, Laurence, he don't do much.
Q What does Mr Hyde do?
A He's Chancellor.
Q He's an important man then?
A Oh yes. There's talk of him having a title. I've heard talk. I get to know little things.
Q What's he going to be called?
A Clarendon. Lord Clarendon.

If we are indeed listening to a reincarnation it is not surprising that the name Laurence Hyde springs into memory as he was a close friend of Nell Gwynn for many years and was a witness to her will. He was the eldest son of Edward Hyde, Earl of Clarendon, Lord Chancellor of England from 1660 to 1667 when he was forced to flee the country in an upsurge of popular feeling at the disastrous naval war with the Dutch. This is one of the very few occasions indeed when Edna-Nell's chronology is at fault: Hyde had been made Lord Clarendon in 1661 – twelve years before Nell said his title was impending – and at the time when she was supposed to be speaking he had already been in exile for six years.

Nell Gwynn's early life is shadowy: a horoscope compiled by Elias Ashmole, the eccentric who founded the Ashmolean Museum in Oxford, shows that she was born on 2 February 1650, but unfortunately we do not know where. Hereford, Oxford and London all lay claim to the honour but none, on the evidence available, can be certain. Edna-Nell was quite definite when she had been taken to the age of four and was in London.

Q How long have you been in London?
A Not very long.
Q And where did you come from?
A (*long pause*) Don't think … I don't think I can say it very well.
Q Come on, try. Try to say it.
A (*Pause, then very slowly*) Herr … ford …

Nell Gwynn's father, Thomas, had been a captain in the Royalist army but with Parliament's victory had fallen on hard times – a situation no doubt

Nell Gwynn's Horoscope which was charted by Elias Ashmole, the founder of the Ashmolean Museum, Oxford

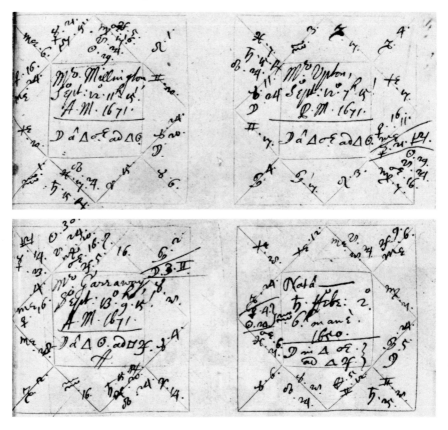

helped by her mother, Ellen or Eleanor Gwynn, who was addicted to brandy and bawdry. There was an older sister, Rose, but no other surviving family. Edna-Nell reports this:

Q What was your father's name?
A Thomas.
Q What does he do?
A He don't do nuffink now.
Q What did he used to do?
A (*immense childish pride*) *My daddy* … he told me … he was a sojer man … he was … a captain sojer man. But he didn't get killed, 'cos he comed 'ome.

When Nell was very small the Gwynns seem to have settled in Coal Yard Alley, a filthy tunnel in the notorious Drury Lane district. Thomas soon vanished from the scene and out of history, though there is a tradition that he died in prison at Oxford. Whether or not the real Nell was disillusioned by her father, Edna-Nell certainly was:

Q Where is your father now?
A Dunno. Me mother ses 'e's bleedin' lazy idle loafer …

With her mother working as barmaid and probably part-time whore in one of the local brothels, and with sister Rose seemingly apprenticed to a similar line, the little Nell Gwynn was left much to her own devices, and almost certainly roamed the streets and alleys. If Edna is anything to judge by, the girl picked up the language and attitudes of the gutter easily enough: when taken on one occasion to the age of seven, her voice immediately became coarse and strident – the epitome of the cheeky little brat.

Q You are Nell Gwynn with all the memories of a seven-year-old. Where are you?
A (*instantly in a coarse voice*) I'm sellin' bleedin' fish.
Q How much do you charge?
A (*shouting out stridently ignoring Keeton*) Fresh 'errings … *thrippence …fresh 'errings … thrippence.*
Q You don't sell many at threepence do you?
A Shut yer bleedin' mouth. (*calling out*) *Thrippence … thrippence … thrippence.*
Q Where do you get them?
A (*pause*) Eeeeee. I think Kate [i.e. Rose] gets 'em me. I didn't get them.
Q Yes, but where does she get them?
A I don't bleedin' know where she gets 'em. (*calling out*) *Fresh herrings? thrippence … do you want fresh herrings, lady … Yes, I've just chopped their bleedin' heads off …* (*pause then in the normal conversational voice to Keeton*) She bought a bleedin' 'errin'.

Nell was known to have sold fish on the streets

There is nothing here that adds materially to the historical knowledge of Nell Gwynn, but it is interesting to note that some years later when her star was in the ascendant at court, Lord Rochester wrote a scurrilous poem about the upstart from the slums:

> Whose first employment was, with open throat,
> To cry fresh herrings, e'en at ten a groat ...

At some time before she was ten the real Nell Gwynn gravitated to the tavern-brothel where her mother worked, running errands, serving drinks and it may be anything that might add a piquancy to customers with specialized interest. Edna-Nell, taken to the age of eight, gave the following:

Q What do you do?
A I go to that gin shop over there ... I take gins round.
Q What do they pay you for that?
A They don't pay me nowt – they give it Kate [i.e. her mother]. They say I'm making a bonny lass ...
Q Have you ever had a sip of gin?
A Yes.
Q Do you like it?
A I don't know right (*smacks lips several times, runs tongue over lips not very happily for a few moments*) Catches yer at back of t'throat a bit ...

A year later Edna-Nell had become accustomed to the flavour:

A Sssssssssssssh ... I ... I think ... I'm ... drunk ... I keep ... 'avin' a sup outa one ... then a sup ... out another ... hip ... (*faintly and pathetically*) I ... think ... I'm going to ... be sick.

The physical symptoms were so convincing that she was sent into a deep sleep and told to come forward to another period of her life. There is no doubt that the real Nell and most of the court drank very heavily indeed, and gin may well have contributed to her death at the age of thirty-seven, which was very early even by seventeenth-century standards. Certainly after the age of fourteen the subject of gin comes up in the majority of regressions.

The first real step on the ladder to the top came when Nell Gwynn became an orange girl at the King's Theatre, Drury Lane, most probably through the influence of her sister, Rose, who had some association with Harry Killigrew, son of Thomas Killigrew, courtier, dramatist, manager and owner of the theatre. The theatre had opened in February 1663 after the bleak years of the Commonwealth when dramatic performances were banned. Widow Mary Meggs (Orange Moll) had obtained a licence from the management to sell oranges, fruit and sweetmeats in the auditorium for a payment of six shillings and eight pence a day, and for thirty-nine years ruled with an iron hand. The King's Company at Drury Lane and the Duke's Company at Dorset Garden by the Thames were very much extensions of the court: most of the audiences were hangers-on, plays were written with topical and personal references to the small circle that attended, and the nobles themselves would sometimes take a turn on the stage.

The men who crowded into the pit of the theatre, where one could stand for one shilling and sixpence (Edna-Nell gave this figure and that for the boxes at the back correctly) were a raffish crew, coarse and arrogant even when sober and alone, but in number and slightly tipsy waiting for the play to begin at three in the afternoon, they could be insufferable. Pepys often comments on the 'base company of ': Edna-Nell goes into more detail.

Q Do you like selling oranges?
A No – because you have to go in and out of them all.
Q And what happens then?
A They're always puttin' their hands up yer skirt ... Then they'll go down there ... then they'll hit yer ... then smack yer 'ere ...
Q What do you do?
A If I'm 'andy enough I smack 'em back ... pull their 'air ... bash 'em on t'nose ...

No doubt it was in the theatre that the real Nell as well as Edna/Nell first came into contact with the gentlemen and their ladies as well. At fourteen, Edna-Nell still feels much in awe as she whispers 'His Majesty ... Me lady ... Mr Pippy (Pepys)' but it is not many years before these are 'Charlie', 'lady whore Castlemaine', and plain Pippy.

Nell Gwynn's career as an actress was longer than that of the orange girl, but it was still brief: her first appearance on the stage was in the spring of 1665 when she was just fifteen and her last in 1671. Of these six years, the theatres were closed for seventeen months because of the plague by order of the Lord Chamberlain, and Nell was absent for about six months in 1669–70 because of the birth of her first son by the King.

As this period of her life is the best documented with facts from play bills, theatrical records and critical comments on her abilities and activities by Pepys and others it seems important to explore it fully to establish not only the validity of Edna but also of the whole phenomenon of regression.

There were hopes of hearing speeches from plays, anecdotes of players, details of costume, sidelights on production, records of all of which are sketchy. But if Nell Gwynn was the 'taunting, teasing jade' described by one of her contemporaries not entirely in sympathy with her, this quality certainly comes through Edna-Nell, however she is producing the material. We get half-glimpses as she flicks aside momentarily the curtain of ignorance – and then lets it fall more darkly than before because of what might have been. Edna's regressions are exhilarating, disappointing, revealing, tantalizing: at some times she is playing to the crowd as did the original, giving the strident, boisterous bawdy answers that amuse, while at others she is intent, serious and obviously genuinely worried that she cannot supply the answer to the question that has been asked.

Samuel Pepys. Nell mentions Pepys (Pippy) frequently and it is clear from his Diary that Pepys admired Nell

As the Restoration Theatre drew its clientele from the very limited circle of the court and high fashion, faces tended to appear several times each week, and plays had to be changed virtually daily. Actors were forced to learn lines rapidly: production seems minimal and ad-libbing was a universal necessity. Performances seem to have been enlivened – or destroyed – by frequent exchanges between cast and audience, many of whom were on very familiar terms in the auditorium, the changing rooms and the bedroom.

Nell Gwynn was illiterate: several of her letters to James II asking for financial help still exist – they are written by an amanuensis and Nell has scrawled a crude unformed 'E.G.' at the bottom. In one regression an imaginary letter was said to have been written and Edna-Nell asked to sign it: she made a very loose 'E.G.' in the air, and not the N.G. expected. Because she could not read, one questioner asked her how she learned her long parts in the plays.

A Charles Hart taught me how to learn my parts – he's a *good* actor, and when I was acting he used to have me for *hours* ... and *hours*, goin' over it ... Have you ever done that?

Q No, I haven't.

A He'd start in the morning and by four o'clock in the afternoon I had to know every word.

Q Oh, I see.

A Now then ... and I did it ... Mind you ... if I missed a word or two I could put in me own then.

Q That's right.

A And them down there didn't know ... they thought it were all part of the play until they heard it done properly ... but you see, I *can't* do it properly.

If this is some element of the actress Nell Gwynn speaking, the learning process must have made a deep impression for she refers to it again and again throughout the regressions. On one occasion she describes Dryden's annoyance at her making up the lines, and on another how Killigrew threatened to dismiss her because she had not learned her part correctly.

These are typical extracts from Edna-Nell's theatrical period; in the following she was eighteen:

Q Come forward a few hours. You are actually in the play. What are you playing?

A I'm not on all the bleedin' time. I'm stood here ... I've been on and I've come off.

Q But what is the play called?

A I'm Lady Wealthy ... I can't remember the name of the play.

Q Find out – ask someone else. They are all in it. Are you enjoying it?

A No ... I don't like this ...

It is surprising that Edna-Nell cannot remember 'The English Monsieur' by James Howard as the comedy part of Lady Wealthy was one of Nell Gwynn's greatest triumphs. Because she could not recall it she used one of her usual evasion techniques of saying how much she would have liked to play Miranda in 'The Tempest', but this time there was a new twist:

A An' I'll tell you another one you'd like ...

Q What's that?

A Now that one's funny ... 'Macbeth'. (*declaims in a strident voice*) Begone thou bloody stain ... (*ordinary voice*) I'd do that.

Q I'm sure you could. Who said that?

A A queen ... she's gorra stain on 'er 'and ... she's killed ... wait a minute ... her 'usband ... *no*, she didn't ... she killed a king ... She killed a king ... No, she didn't. *Somebody* killed a king an' she 'ad summat to do with it ...

Nell was known especially for her roles in comedy

Q Yes?

A An' she got some blood on 'er 'and and she says *'Begone thou stain'* (*anticlimax*) or summat like that ... Woe ... *woe.*

Of the hundreds of plays that Nell Gwynn must have seen or acted in Edna-Nell remembers only a handful. Apart from the two by Shakespeare and Dryden's 'Maiden Queen', she names only 'The Indian Emperor' and 'The Indian Queen', both by Dryden and which not unnaturally she confuses – sometimes they appear as Indian Empress or Indian Princess or once Emperor's Wife. In the next extract Edna-Nell was also in the theatre, but this time in the audience. Her mind tries desperately to reconcile the character talking to the unseen questioner with the reality of being surrounded by other people who cannot understand the situation:

A I'm at the theatre ... but I'm not watching, am I? I'm talkin' to you ... y'know, I think I'm fuddled wi' gin.

Q Why?

A Well, here I am talkin' and there they are knowing I'm talkin', but they can't see you ... They'll think I'm doin' the play, won't they, because I used to act in this one y'know.

Q Did you? What is it called, this play?

A T'Emperor's Wife ... now in that play, y'see, they have a daughter and they're trying to get her married to somebody, an' she don't want to be married to 'im ... now what's 'er name ... *Sadria* ... the name of the daughter, Sadria ... 'an that's what I used to be but people said I were no good in it.

Q Why?

A Because it's tragedy, an' I'm no good in tragedy because when they see me dying on the stage I 'ave to giggle ...

The real Nell Gwynn did play the part of Cydaria in 'The Indian Emperor' – it was her first role, and as she said, a disaster. There may be some confusion with the part of Samira which she played in 'The Surprizal'.

Of the characters in the theatre Edna-Nell mentions only Mrs Knipp, Charles Hart, and Becky Marshall, all of the King's Company, and Moll Davis who was also one of Charles' mistresses, of the Duke's.

One of the most intriguing extracts of the theatrical sequences is Edna-Nell's description of 'The Tempest' costumes: if only we could rely on this it would be an extremely valuable contribution to the history of the theatre of the time.

Q What other parts are there? [In addition to Miranda]

A There's the father ... an' there's Ariel ...

Q There's an ugly man in the play ... a kind of monster, isn't there?

A (*very excited – face lights up*) Ooooh ... yes ... I can't think of his name ... but I can see him.

Q How did they dress him at the Duke's then?

A They put ... a wig on him ... (*revulsion*) *Uggggh* ... it were all dirty and stuck out. (*mimes*)

Q Was there any paint on his face?

A Yes, it were across here (*draws hand across eyes*) an' they put something on his nose to make it all big an' lumpy ... and something round 'ere (*indicates mouth*) to make his mouth all 'orrible.

Q What clothes was he wearing, Nell?

A He 'ad a short green thing ... an' hose ... an' he had a belt round 'im 'ere ... in points ... all the way round like that.

Q What was the father dressed like?

A He 'ad a long robe on like that ... it was like ... a black one ... an' it fell in folds to the floor ... And he 'ad a collar that doubled over ... and it came right down the front ... 'e 'ad a beard, but not a lot of paint on 'is face.

Q Have you remembered that monster's name yet?

A C ... Cabal ... no ... C ... C ... Cab ... Cal ... No ... can't remember it.

Again one of Edna-Nell's near misses: she could not remember Caliban, but it is interesting to see that she mentioned the word 'Cabal' which at the time would have been the group of five ministers running the country.

In one late regression when Edna-Nell had been talking about her life of luxury as a royal mistress freely Keeton suddenly sent her into a deep sleep and told her to come to the time when she was actually on the stage acting: it was, he said, the very end of the play.

Q What are you doing?

A I come to the front an' stand there ... I'm going to say (*clears throat loudly*)
My ladies and my gentlemen, it does not seem
To be quite the thing, for you have seen
Poor Nelly die – an' spring to life again.
How can it be ... But I am here
I hope you have all enjoyed the play,
You'll come again the morrow
But I shan't die ... for I am here
To play the comedy – on the morrow.
Farewell my friends, Remember Charles and Nelly
Not forgetting Madge – you'll buy your oranges from Madge.

It does not bear much resemblance to the epilogue to 'Tyrannic Love' quoted on page 157 which it is obviously supposed to be, but it is remarkable that unlettered Edna without a moment's hesitation produced the passage.

Nell Gwynn's budding career was cut short after only a few months when the theatres were closed because of the plague (June 1665). What happened to her in the seventeen months is not known: some biographers guess that she either went with the court fringe to Oxford, or to the country where she lived with Charles Hart. If Edna-Nell is correct, she did neither.

Edna suggests that Nell stayed in London during the plague but did not venture out

Q Where is your father now?
A Don't know ... he could have died when all that disease was about.
Q You didn't get it?
A I stopped in ... Katy Rose went and got what we wanted.
Q So you and your mother stayed indoors?
A No. Katy Rose and Katy Ellen went and got what we wanted but I didn't go out.
Q Where was this you stayed in? Was it in London?
A In Leckoner Lane.
Q What about the theatres?
A Ah. Them were closed.

'Leckoner Lane' is almost certainly Lewkenor Lane (now Macklin Street) but then a filthy alley off Drury Lane renowned for its brothels. It was in Madame Ross's establishment in Lewkenor Lane that the young Nell Gwynn probably worked for a while as a serving maid.

For an event as traumatic as the Great Plague, which must have struck the ultimate terror into the heart of every Londoner, Edna/Nell gives nothing but the stereotyped picture that every schoolchild knows.

A Court's movin' ... down to Hampton.
Q Because of the plague? Are you going with them?
A Don't know.

Q What do they do with the bodies?
A (*long pause*) They ... just ... push them onto carts. They shout ... shout in t'streets ... They ring.
Q They ring and they shout? What do they shout?
A (*strident*) *Bring out your dead* ... (*quieter*) Bring out your dead ... (*a frightened whisper*) Bring out ... your dead.
Q Then do they have to fetch them out?
A Then they have to take t'dead out ... and they *throw* 'em on the cart ... with everybody else's dead ... and (*long pause*) I ... I ... think they bury 'em.

Her description of the Great Fire of London in the following year (1666) is even more trite:

A *Everything's gone.*
Q Where did it start?
A In a baker's shop ...
Q I know, but where was the baker's shop?
A (*long pause*) Oh ... on Pudding Lane.
Q Do they all say it was Pudding Lane? I've heard some say it was somewhere else?
A Nooooo ... they said it were a baker's ... Hodgons ... (*doubtfully*) Hodgsons ... H ... Hodgsons ... bakery ... he makes bread on Pudding Lane ... Hodgson ... everything's gone ...

On another occasion she mentioned the hackneyed anecdotes of the King and Duke of York supervising the operations and of the Lord Mayor ordering houses to be blown up as a firebreak, but as the apparently unstoppable fire swept to within 800 metres of where Nell Gwynn lived, Edna-Nell's accounts seem inspired more by conscious than unconscious memories.

Soon after the theatres opened in 1667 came the Buckhurst episode: Nell Gwynn became his mistress and went to live at his house in Epsom for a few months, and a mock marriage service was arranged. Pepys writes on 13 July 1667: 'Mr Pierce tells what troubles me that my Lord Buckhurst hath got Nell away from the King's house, and gives her £100 a year and so she has sent her parts back to the house and will act no more ...' Edna-Nell does not put it quite so delicately: ''E gives me 'undred pounds fer lyin' on me back ...'

Nell was back at the theatre before the end of 1677, a sadder, wiser girl: Pepys writes (26 August): '... Nell is already left Lord Buckhurst ... and swears she hath had all she could get of him: and Hart (i.e. Charles) her great admirer now hates her: and that she is very poor, and hath lost my lady Castlemaine who was her great friend also: but she hath come to the playhouse but is neglected by them all ...' Apart from a brief reference, Edna-Nell skips this unhappy period:

A Me 'an Buckhurst went down to – you may know it – Epsom – they have horse games there … well, me an' Buckhurst went down there … it were only for sport … I reckoned to marry him … I didn't marry him … it were … sport. Anyway I lived with 'im, but not for long …

Soon the vivacious Nell was edging her way into the fringe of the court circle, and within a couple of years to the very centre. Of the scores of hours of regression of this period the majority is inconsequential chatter, and generally when Edna-Nell seems to sense the questioning is getting too specific she resorts to gin.

Q You are now twenty … where are you Nell?
A I … I … I jus' … hadda lil' … drink.
Q What are you doing?
A I … I … I …
Q Where do you live now?
A I … I … in … bottom of *Pell Mell* … *I've* had a little … drink … an' ah'm gonna … 'ave … anuzzer … lil' … drink …

The only points of interest in this incoherent babble is the specific pro-nunciation *Pell Mell* instead of the modern Pall Mall – the street was named after the seventeenth-century ball game pell-mell. Thomas Blount (1670) says: 'This game was heretofore used in the long alley near St James, and vulgarly called Pell-Mell.'

Much of Edna-Nell's talk at this period concerns her rivals – a topic which no doubt occupied a great deal of the real Nell Gwynn's time as well. Barbara Villiers-Lady Castlemaine, who had been the King's main mistress and who had borne him four or five children, could afford to be generous, as Pepys said, to the actress from the gutter as long as she remained in her place on the stage, but when she began to sidle towards the King's bedroom, 'Me Lady' as the younger Nell called her, began to feel the weight of her extra ten years and six children. There was considerable hostility between the two at court, both historically and in regression. Edna-Nell snaps, '… me lady whore …' or '… she's a pig …' She accuses Castlemaine of spying on everyone else in the court and flying into terrible rages until the King gave her what she wanted. And it is certain that the historical Barbara Villiers for a number of years wielded immense power behind the scenes in all aspects of running the state. Her influence had, however, almost gone by 1674 when the beautiful, greedy and unscrupulous Breton, Louise de Kéroualle, had become the King's chief mistress. Louise had come to England with Charles' sister, Henrietta, Duchess of Orleans – or Minette as he called her – in 1670 when a French mission had arrived to arrange the secret Treaty of Dover. Although Louise returned to France a few weeks later, Charles soon had her appointed as maid-of-honour to Queen Catherine, and very rapidly completed the process of seduction. Although historically the chief rivalry was now between Louise and Nell Gwynn, there does seem

Charles II. He is reputed to have said on his deathbed, 'Let not poor Nellie starve'

to have been something of a truce between Nell and Lady Castlemaine in the face of opposition. Edna-Nell wherever she gets the material from, reports the progress accurately:

A Me lady's bin right nice to me lately.
Q Why?
A Because … you've not seen Squintabel have you? [Louise de Kéroualle had a slight cast in one eye] You've not seen Squintabel have you?
Q Who's Squintabel?
A You've not seen 'er? Well … Minette come, an' she brought Squintabel with 'er.
Q Who's Squintabel?
A I can't say it – but she took 'er back with 'er, but everybody knows Charles' eyes were on 'er. Now me lady's bin nice to me …

The other woman who occupied much of Edna-Nell's time – always with immense sympathy and regard – is the lovely Frances Stewart, one of the King's failures. He tried desperately to make Frances his mistress, but despite everything she resisted even though he had her installed in the Palace. Eventually, still unsubdued she eloped in the night, married and later became the Duchess of Richmond. The year after her marriage (1668) she contracted smallpox and was heavily disfigured: forgiven, she returned to court where she remained until well after Charles' death.

Edna-Nell reported all of these facts more or less correctly and then added an anecdote which one would love to prove. She claims that she helped to save Frances when the King was most passionate and determined.

A King wanted her for his mistress an' she didn't want it.
Q Yes?
A I ... *no* ... I didn't ... no names ... but *somebody* put some jallop in his drink.
Q What for?
A And instead of getting upstairs he got where he wanted to have a shit in one of them new closets ... So ...
Q What happened then?
A So ... everybody came runnin' because they thought he had fallen down the stairs, an' she sighed with relief. ... she would do, would Frances ... she'd go Aaaaaa.

It is interesting that when Edna-Nell was asked where she had obtained the 'jallop' she said that it was an apothecary named Lorner or Loyner: Nell Gwynn's physician and in her later years a personal friend was Richard Lower.

When Charles' last major mistress, the Italian Hortense Mancini, Duchess of Mazarin, arrived in England in 1675 with the deliberate intention of seducing him, Nell Gwynn was probably secure in her own little niche – a coarse, boisterous but warm refuge for the King from the artificial court. Edna-Nell refers to her only occasionally and rather obscurely: 'There's a new one ... Mon ... Mont ... Montspellier ... or something like that.'

It is rather disappointing that of all of the hundreds of people Nell Gwynn must have met, so few names appear in the regressions, and these very random. There are single and vague references to Prince Rupert, Lord Wilmot and Lord Meredith, and once Edna-Nell says, 'Mr Childs pays me me money ...' Childs was the real Nell's banker.

Brought to the age of thirty-four (1684, the year before Charles' death) she was asked what news there was in the court and a sudden flurry of names appeared:

A (*very seriously*) Charles is not so well ... not been well for a bit.
Q What is the matter – what form does the illness take?
A They bleed 'im.

Q Who does that?
A Tenison ... an' there's another one ... Lowler? Lowner?
Q Are you sure the name is Tenison?
A Well, Tenison is there ... I can't go in y'see ...

The Lowler or Lowner could be the Dr Lower mentioned earlier, perhaps confused with one of the King's doctors, Harel. Dr Thomas Tenison was at the time the very fashionable minister at St Martin's-in-the-Fields, and later Archbishop of Canterbury, who towards the end of Nell Gwynn's life became a close friend and who conducted her funeral service. Probed further on Charles' illness she said he had had a great deal of trouble:

A There was all that bother not so long ago.
Q What was that?
A Over ... somebody called ... Oates ... Tit ... ius ... no ... Titus ... Oates, an' they said Monmouth ... an' there were some others ... an' they were going to kill Charles and James.
Q What happened to Titus Oates?
A He was ... up in front of the judges.

The Titus Oates plot (1678–80) purported to show by a whole series of faked documents that the Catholics were intending to assassinate Charles and to install Monmouth in his place. Anti-Catholic feelings were powerful for a time, but subsided when the whole falsity of the accusations were revealed. Oates, despite savage treatment in prison, survived until well into the next century, living on a government pension. There was one strange comment associated with this incident which appeared in a much later regression. The original Oates depositions were heard by a magistrate, Sir Edmund Godfrey, whose murdered body was found soon after at Hampstead and although three men were executed for the crime, it is generally thought that they were completely innocent. Once when asked if there was any news, Edna-Nell said right out of context:

A There's a man ... a judge ... G ... G ... Go ... God ... bin murdered ... and they've hanged three men ... at Tyburn.

Edna-Nell shows the typical name confusion under hypnosis in spite of her long experience: she refers once to a bed designed by 'Mr Jones ... 'e's gorra funny name Impetigo ...' She struggles on several occasions to get the name of the painter Lely, but never succeeds.

Q What about that man you said drew pictures of Villiers? What was his name? You never told us.
A You never asked.
Q I'll bet they were nice pictures to look at, weren't they?
A He draws a picture of her ... sometimes she has no clothes on, an' some-

times she's only a little bit on ... now what's 'is name ... Lyes? ... Nase?
Leys – summat like that.

Q Have you ever had your picture painted?

A I was goin' to tell you that ... Leys painted it.

Q And were you naked?

A No ... I don't uncover myself ... I sat like that (*poses*)

Q Have you ever seen a picture of a lady lying down naked with two little
angels?

A Yes ... Charles has one ... that's me lady.

Whether or not it is the heightened sense of morality under hypnosis, Edna-
Nell is always adamant that despite the nude Lely portrait in the Bowes
Collection she did not take off her clothes to be painted. She maintains that
the face and clothes are hers, but the body is someone else's.

Nell Gwynn by Simon Verlest

Apart from Charles and perhaps Barbara Villiers the name Pepys occurs more frequently than any other: 'he works for t'government' – later she specifies 'for th'Admiralty but he don't wear a uniform'. 'He does a lotta writin''; 'Pippy struts when 'e walks'; 'Pippy's goin' blind ...'; he is always at the theatre where, if he gets the chance ''e smacks ladies' behinds'; 'Pippy's serious – 'is wife keeps 'im serious'; There are many references to Mrs Pepys too: 'Elizabeth Pippy is always ill'; ''is wife don't know about 'im and Knipps ...'; 'Pippy's wife is dead ... and she were only twenty-nine'; ''is wife talks a bit like Louise'. Elizabeth Pepys was always ailing, and did have considerable trouble with Samuel's extra-marital adventures: she died when she was twenty-nine, and as the daughter of a French refugee family may well have had an accent like that of Louise de Kéroualle.

It could be said that in these many hours of regression by sheer coincidence some facts would be correct, but it is difficult to see how such specific material as the following sequence, which suddenly came out in the middle of one of the Lady Castlemaine tirades, can be mere chance.

A I *know* ... I know what you'd like to know.
Q What's that?
A I told you about Frances ... Frances Stewart – didn't I? Well ... Charles *decided* he'd 'ave a new (*gropes for the word*) ... a new coin ... an *half* penny ... a new half penny ... an' Frances is on the back of it ... she's sat there 'oldin' something up ... an' something on 'er 'ead ... 'an she's sat there.

The new halfpenny of 1672 carried for the first time on the reverse the traditional figure of Britannia, for which Frances Stewart was indeed the model.

When Edna-Nell was brought to the age of thirty-five, she was in paroxysms of grief, for Charles was dying: her greatest agony she said was that they would not let her in to see him for the last time – and it is correct that as a matter of decency none of the mistresses was admitted. Six of the 'royal bastards' including Nell Gwynn's surviving son were all brought in to receive their father's blessing – though Edna-Nell, too wrapped in her own grief, does not mention this.

After the death of Charles, Nell Gwynn was in poor financial straits as her regular allowance ceased. As her creditors closed in she appealed to James II for help and even if the famous last words of Charles – 'Let not poor Nelly starve' – were never really uttered, the new king did settle her debts and give her some money. But having been accustomed to high living, Nell found it difficult to retract and was soon forced to sell her valuables, especially the wonderful pearl necklace she had bought from the actress and mistress of Prince Rupert, Peg Hughes. Edna-Nell commented on this: 'I sold it to the jeweller ... the man you buy jewels from ... No, I didn't ... I sold it to the man who made me bed (Nell Gwynn is reported as having a bed made of silver) – I paid four thousand and some 'undreds of pounds for me necklace but I didn't get that much.'

By November 1687 it was obvious that Nell Gwynn was dying, paralysed in part of her body: her kinder friends attributed her illness to apoplexy, the realists to the pox. By the 14th she was dead, and three days later was buried at St Martin's.

Edna-Nell was switched from the middle of one of her boisterous extrovert youthful sequences suddenly and without any warning:

Q Come to the last moments of Nell Gwynn ... The last things that Nell Gwynn remembers ... Where are you, Nell?
A (*very weak, and feeble, only just audible*) In ... bed.
Q What is the matter? (*silence*) What *is* the matter, Nell?
A Can't ... move.
Q Why, what has happened?
A (*more faintly*) Do you ... think ... it's ... time ...
Q Time for what?
A (*silence for ten seconds, then almost inaudible*) S'time ... I ... spoke ... th'epilogue ... ?
Q What is the epilogue? (*silence*) Do you remember it? (*silence*) Try to remember the epilogue, Nell ... Do try ...

Nothing more could be obtained from Edna-Nell, but when she was wakened up she said that when she was asked what the epilogue was four lines rushed into her mind, though she could not produce them under hypnosis. Afterwards she recalled the words:

> Oh but to stay a little while
> To live and whore if only till we tire,
> But faith I shan't be gone for long,
> For I'll be back again.

To regress to a well-documented historical character must always seem to some people to be suspicious – it is just too easy they say to learn up the correct facts and to produce them under hypnosis, even if they are not consciously deceiving. But as every person who has regressed will testify this just cannot be done: they know certain material, but they just cannot say it and all the learned facts sit imprisoned, silent and helpless at the back of the mind while the unknown rushes free. The whole process is so different from the normal waking state that even if Edna Greenan had read the whole of Pepys, several biographies of Nell Gwynn and many history texts on the social and political background, she still may not have been capable of producing a single fact from them unless some other, and unknown, factor was operating. And everyone who knows Edna is adamant that she has never read a single book on the subject at all.

Can Edna really have some element of Nell Gwynn in her present being? Mathematically, of course, the chances of any known character reappearing in the minute sample of the population as a whole that Keeton has regressed must be billions to one, and the odds of a historical personality whose character is in one way or another so relevant to the subject's own, is even more remote. Yet people do win the jackpot in a giant lottery at their first attempt – and with a single ticket.

So, one must accept that reincarnation, if it exists at all, is a possibility: the incredibly strict chronology of Edna-Nell's regression seems to support the theory, but the triviality of much of the material, as always, seems to refute it, particularly as Nell Gwynn's life was so full, so variable and so packed with powerful memories of people and events.

If ancestral memory can be applied at all, then Nell Gwynn is an ideal subject, for today, three centuries after her death there must be hundreds of people alive with some Gwynn-Stuart blood in their veins, and who can say that Edna is not one of them, even if it could never be proved? Nell's surviving son had twelve children from his marriage to Diane de Vere, daughter of the Earl of Oxford, and who can tell what side branches appeared in succeeding generations: dominant genes are not particular which bed saw their beginning. Again the usual problem remains: Nell's son was born in 1670 when one presumes acquired memoires were transmitted, and yet Edna/Nell has a great deal to say about the last seventeen years of her life. Nevertheless, ancestral memory could be a factor for the earlier years of Nell Gwynn's life.

Cosmic memory too may be a possibility: it may be that additions to the store made by strong emotions or by individuals of powerful personality may have some distinctive element that makes them more easily selected by certain subjects, just as feeling in the darkness in a sack of identical balls, they could quickly select the single cube.

Telepathy as we generally recognize it may be a factor, as in the Orrery-Otway incident described on page 21, but it seems to be only very marginally involved if at all. Much of the material produced under regression was not known by anyone present, and conversely most of that which was familiar to everyone – that Charles' wife was Catherine of Braganza, for example, and not Anne-Marie – Edna-Nell failed completely to get.

Even the subconscious which in many regressions seems to be a kind of safety net for sceptics lets us down, for knowing Edna's background and tastes, there just seems no way in which she could ever, either consciously or unconsciously, have heard or read of the obscure detail of political and social life of the seventeenth century that appears in every regression. Edna then, remains perhaps the most enigmatic of all the regressions unless one accepts more or less whole-heartedly that some element of the immensely strong personality that was once Eleanor Gwynn is now embedded in Edna Greenan. Is it significant that their initials are the same?

8. Continuous Existences?

Frances Isaacson

One very interesting aspect of regression is that many – perhaps most – subjects can recall what seems to be several lives, often running consecutively, and every hypnotist working in this field must dream of finding in one of these existences a character who can speak a language or perform some task such as playing a musical instrument, which the person cannot do in his everyday life. This would seem on the face of it to be a fairly conclusive proof of reincarnation, but unfortunately the occasions on which it occurs are very, very rare indeed, and even then when the circumstances are examined closely there are often factors which lead one to suspect a less dramatic but still remarkable explanation. Nevertheless, to watch a subject who at one moment is conversing freely with the group and the next is quite genuinely unable to understand a word they are saying is very impressive.

Keeton was confronted with this dramatic situation in what were literally his last hours in the United States. In a third and final session with

Frances Isaacson, a sixty-year-old craft teacher who had already regressed to
two American-born personalities, he was suddenly faced with a character
who could not comprehend a single question that was asked her in English.

The whole series had been dogged by frustrations and accidents from a
point of view of checking out the material historically but they were interesting in showing what might be a continuous flow of existence, right into
Frances' present life. If reincarnation or some persistence of memory is the
reason for the phenomenon of regression then a series of existences seems
logical enough for it would be arrogant to believe that the present life and
one other were the only ones through which an individual passes. If, however, regression stems from some functioning of the unconscious mind the
successive personalities are more difficult to explain because the temperaments one subject adopts are often completely different. One would expect
some uniformity, or at least common element, unless of course the conflicting
characters are different aspects of the same person.

Frances' opening remarks in her first regression were unusually clear and
prompt with at first only occasional hesitations about names and dates.

Q Who are you?
A Margaret.
Q How old are you? Do you know the year?
A 1811.
Q Are you grown up or small?
A I'm small ... eleven.

This immediate and free response was kept up for several minutes, and it
was established that the family name was Benson, that her mother was dead
and that her father was a merchant who sold dishes, pots, pans and yardage:
'yardage' was one of those strange words that slipped out involuntarily,
and much to the amazement of the conscious mind. Frances says she was
completely unaware of its use as a synonym for 'fabric' or 'material'.
Margaret Benson said that she lived in Grosvenor Square, but would not
give a town or even a country. After this there was a frustrating series of
'Don't knows' and silences, and as up to this point all the questioning had
been done by Joe Keeton himself, it was suspected that the unfamiliar
British accent might be inhibiting replies. An American voice took over, and
immediately the answers came more fluently.

Q Do you know what state you are in?
A New Hampshire.
Q That's a nice state – which town?
A Concord.

She then named a Lucy McDougall who was her friend, a Mr Bartholomew
who was either a teacher or pastor, and said that she herself lived in Beacon
(or Deacon) Street. Most of the people she knew were connected with

farming, but there was a place which made shoes. Once again there came a spell of silences or non-committal replies, and as Margaret's knowledge of the locality seemed to have been exhausted she was brought on to the age of twenty-one.

Instantly the limited eleven-year-old turned into a small-minded, bourgeois snob, about to be married.

Q Where are you?
A I'm in church. I'm wearing a white dress and I'm going to be married.
Q Who are you marrying?
A Richard … Smith … (*pause, then sharply and tartly*) With a 'Y'. Smyth.
Q Has anything of importance been happening recently?
A I've been putting up fruit.
Q What does your husband do?
A (*smugly, and with a conceited expression on her face*) He's a doctor.
Q Where did he qualify as a doctor? [This point was pressed several times]
A (*hesitantly*) Reid … College? Reid? I think it's in Canada.

As so often when a subject is under pressure to provide an answer which does not come to the unconscious, there may well have been some conscious prompting to the last question: Frances lives about 300 kilometres north of Portland, Oregon, where there is today a Reid College with which as a teacher she is familiar. The 'Canada' is more significant.

From then on Margaret Smyth's life ran the dreary but very consistent pattern that is characteristic of so many regressions and which highlights the problems of trying to find a satisfactory explanation for them. If there is

A general view of Concord, New Hampshire in the nineteenth century

a survival of anything at all – spirit, soul, memory or consciousness – why should it be largely the trivia of routine rather than traumatic experiences? Why should the 'eternal' part of a Margaret remember the colour of one dress, bottling fruit, sitting in a rocking chair or dusting when even the dreariest life must have some moments of intense drama? As she says that four children survived, there was probably one that died, and in any case there must have been serious illnesses that would torment any mother – yet there are no references, not even of her husband's death apart from one passing and unemotional comment.

Can the explanation be that we are wrong to expect the regressed character to have a memory of the same kind and functioning in the same way as the subject's waking one? Perhaps the secret of questioning is to take the subject to the exact moment when the event is happening before they can describe it in any detail at all – and as even the most exciting life is more than ninety-nine per cent dull routine the chance of hitting the precise moment is very remote. At thirty-one Margaret Smyth is deep in her narrow rut: she says she lives at Oak Lane, Concord, and has three children. If one *had* to buy a dress ('my housekeeper makes *mine*') she thinks it would cost about

Victorian women 'putting up' fruit jelly

55. The only national news she can think of – and that only because it involves a friend – is that many men are going west to find vacant land. Preoccupied with her house and family she has little idea who her husband's patients are, but says that he deals largely with kicks from horses. She does not help in the dispensary ('my husband calls it his laboratory') but does know that there is a yellowish-brown mixture for stomach upsets (probably kaolin-opium), iodine for cuts and Epsom salts for unspecified troubles.

At forty she is found, full of weariness, in a rocking chair and sighs with the classic mid-marriage disillusionment in full flood: if this is the memory of a real person in the 1840s then feelings have not changed much – it is only that now the social and legal climate allows partners more easily to make a fresh start elsewhere in the elusive hope of doing better the second time round.

Q Where are you?
A (*utterly weary and fed up*) Still in the *same* house.
Q You sound tired – what is the matter?
A Too much work.
Q Is your husband still alive?
A Yes.
Q Does he look after you?
A Too busy.
Q Don't you still have servants?
A Mmmm.
Q Then you shouldn't be tired. Why are you tired?
A Children (*deep sighs*).

At sixty things seemed over the hump, but whether this was due to maturity or resignation there was no hint: nevertheless, responses were livelier than at any other period of her life.

Q Where are you?
A Dusting.
Q Are you in good health?
A (*with considerable feeling – a mixture of disgust and the only flash of humour Margaret showed in the whole regression*) *No teeth.*
Q What's been happening in the world? Who is president?
A They're talking about Lincoln.
Q Did you vote for him?
A They don't let us vote … he's gonna free the Negroes.
Q Does that meet with universal approval?
A No.
Q Who is objecting?
A My husband.
Q Why?
A We don't have enough work for the Negroes.

If the dating is correct and this is 1860, it would of course have been the year in which Lincoln was elected, and though franchise for adult males in New Hampshire was liberal by mid-nineteenth-century standards, women in the state did not get the vote until well into the twentieth century. One can well imagine a reactionary and ageing country doctor putting up such an irrational argument against Negro emancipation. Awake, Frances said that she could not have said precisely when Lincoln was elected nor when women in the state were enfranchised.

There are only two more brief sequences with Margaret: at sixty-seven she said her husband had been dead for a year, but showed no particular emotion. He was buried at their church, which had a white steeple and was situated 'just off' the 'Commons', but she was most evasive about the marker or headstone, perhaps because the watchdog in the unconscious felt that there was a possibility it could be checked out. The only real intensity of emotion in the regression came when Margaret was brought to her last moments. The voice became old and frail.

Q How old are you?
A Eighty-nine.
Q There's a good life ... are you afraid?
A Yeh ... not being able to breathe.
Q Tell me, Margaret, who do you think I am?
A (*ignoring the question and obviously muttering to herself*) I don't know what's going ... to happen.
Q What *do* you think happens to people when they die?
A They go to Heaven or (*the voice trails away to awed silence as if rejecting the idea in terror*) or ... Hell.
Q If that is so, why are you afraid?
A (*desperately*) I can't let go. I can't let go ...

The personality disappeared, and no question relating to the doctor's wife from Concord brought out the faintest flicker of response. Frances' head fell to one side as if in normal sleep until Keeton said:

Q It is five years since the death of Margaret. Margaret died five years ago. Where are you?

Immediately a voice very different from the aged woman's of a moment earlier replied in strong childish tones: he said that he was called Randolph and was aged five. Asked what country he lived in, he answered:

A The United States.
Q Which state?
A Virginia.
Q Where in Virginia?
A On a farm ... there's a fence round it ... a white house.

Unfortunately at this point an observer who had never been to a session before asked the character if it knew Richmond, and although Randolph gave the 'Uhuh' with a negative intonation, in later regressions the name of the town cropped up regularly. Names are always difficult to get under hypnosis, and if a subject is offered one, he usually seizes it with gratitude, so that we do not know if Randolph ever did live in Richmond or whether that unfortunate chance comment settled him in a city he never knew. But whatever the truth of the facts, there was no doubt that the same person who a few seconds earlier had been in every way an old, dying woman was now a perky five-year-old.

Q Have you any toys?
A A hammer.
Q Are there any animals around?
A (*delighted*) A ... big ... horse ... he stands there and ... (*with immense pride*) I *brush him*.

At fifteen Randy gives his surname as Nelson, and says that he was born in 1890 and that he is at that moment at a military academy called Briarcliff. He dislikes his school and teachers and says that he 'is not cut out for to be a soldier ...' Virtually nothing of this period is checkable except that one authority reports the existence of a school with a similar name in New York.

At twenty he is back on his father's farm 'racing a horse round the field': although Frances has never had the slightest interest in horses they dominate the life of her Randolph personality and appear in almost every sequence of the regressions:

Q What crops do you grow on the farm? What animals do you have?
A Breed horses ... and hay ... and tobacco ...
Q Where do you sell your tobacco?
A Richmond.
Q Do you know the name of the auctioneer?
A Bress ... Bressler ... Bressler ...
Q Do you remember any statues in Richmond?
A *General* Washington (*particular emphasis on 'General'*).
Q Do you remember where it is?
A In the square ...

Unhappily, the staff of city library in Richmond who have co-operated so well in researching the character of Randolph Nelson have been unable to find any record of an auctioneer named Bressler at this period, nor a family called Nelson. The directories, however, list only residents within the city boundaries and do not include the considerable population in the surrounding counties of Henrico and Chesterfield. There is, of course, a very famous statue of Washington in the centre of the city, but there is no special emphasis on the military aspect of his career. If the place really is named

Richmond, there are at least eighteen to choose from in the United States, and in one session Randy says completely out of context that the address of his home is Needham – there is a Needham in Massachusetts as well as in Virginia.

As 1917 was such a crucial year in American history, Randy was brought forward to the age of twenty-seven: true to form, he was riding towards the barn and when he had bedded down the horse he was prepared to talk.

Q Is there a war on?
A (*emphatically*) No. [In view of his next answer he obviously interpreted this in the light of the US involvement.]
Q Are there wars anywhere?
A Yes ... in Europe.

Brought forwards another six months Randy said that he was at that moment talking to his father.

Q What are you saying?
A We're talking about the war.
Q Has it started yet?
A Not yet.

Randy gave the date as the end of March – he was certain because his sister was being married the following Sunday – and was quite correct in saying that the US was not at war, though the declaration of hostilities was only a few days away on 6 April.

With his military academy training and his riding skills, Randolph seemed a likely volunteer, and was brought forwards a nominal six months to see if he could give any details of the course of the war.

Q Where are you?
A On a ship ... going to France.
Q That's quick isn't it? What unit are you with?
A 67th Infnatry.
Q And what is your rank?
A First Lieutenant.
Q Do you have an army number?
A 10083 [later he altered this to 82003]
Q Do you know the name of the boat? (*silence*) Do you know the name of the port to which you are sailing? (*silence*) Who is your commander?
A Old Beetle ... Beidel.

The timing here is quite possible, though the brevity of the training seems unusual: troops were moving steadily to Europe and by the end of 1917 almost a quarter of a million had crossed the Atlantic. There certainly was a Major General Biddle who was Acting Chief of Staff in France in 1917–18

American troops disembark from a troop ship in Marseilles

but whether it is he to whom Randy refers or to some more junior officer is a matter for speculation.

The alacrity with which Randolph produces a military number may seem a little suspicious, but in some strange way this does seem to be a very powerful symbol: many men now in their eighties can quote instantly their army numbers from the First World War although they have probably not thought of it for sixty years.

Lieutenant Nelson was told to come forward another six months – that is to about the spring or summer of 1918. Instantly there was a marked change in Frances: her body slumped in the chair and an expression of intense drawn pain came into her face. The voice was weak and laboured.

Q Where are you?
A In hospital.
Q Where?
A In France.
Q What are you doing in France?
A I was wounded.
Q Where?
A In my leg ... shot outa nowhere ...
Q When did you come to France?
A About six months ago.
Q Where did you land?
A Marseilles ... [Everyone present assumed that Marseilles was a mistake and that traffic from the US to Europe entered through the Channel ports, but the official history of the war states '... from the beginning of 1918 Marseilles was a major port of entry, especially for materials.']
Q Whereabouts is this hospital?
A In the country.

Q Whereabouts in the country?
A Ah … ah … Loire.
Q But in which town?
A Orléans.
Q What is the number of this hospital?
A 16th.
Q Is there another word … the 16th something hospital?
A (*very tentatively*) Sacred Heart?

After this the voice became more distressed and weak and finally went silent altogether. Without thinking of anything other than knowing if the character had survived the injury Keeton told him to come forwards five years.

Q Where are you?
A (*A perky, childish voice*) At … home.
Q What is your name?
A Frances …

Mrs Isaacson's daughter leaned forward and said, 'Mum was born in 1918.'

Randy Nelson's geography was much better than Frances Isaacson's: unlike her he knew of the river Loire in France, and that the town of Orléans was firm on its banks. These details and the Marseilles comment made it important to check the very specific army information he had given – if number, rank, name and other facts checked out it would seem that a major

American troops near the front line in France

step forward had been taken in explaining regression. But here was the next setback: virtually the whole of the personnel records of the US forces in the First World War were destroyed when a disastrous fire in 1973 gutted the building in St Louis which housed them. The officials there said that they thought there was a 16th medical unit of some sort in France, and that as the Infantry regiments went through to the nineties there should have been a 67th. Officers of the period, however, did not have numbers, and those of the rankers had six digits. Randy's vague 'Sacred Heart' (Frances is a Lutheran, certainly not Catholic) may be significant as French hospitals and other buildings were frequently given over to their allies.

But the most remarkable moments were yet to come: in a brief ten-minute regression as Joe Keeton was about to leave, Frances was told to go back ... back ... twenty years before the birth of Margaret Benson. Although all of the usual questions were asked, there was no reply: 'Who are you?' 'Where are you?' 'What do you see?' were all greeted with uncomprehending silence even though the alertness of the subject showed that she was hearing clearly. Several languages were tried and when none of these brought any response, Frances' daughter suggested that as her mother's grandparents had come from Scandinavia, a Swedish woman present might try, although she knew her mother did not speak the language.

At the very first words in Swedish an expression of enlightenment spread across Frances' face, and though the replies were at first more nods and grunts than speech, it was obvious that she was understanding everything.

Q Var bor du? Vet du namnet? Är det en by eller stan? (*Where do you live? Do you know the name? Is it a village or a town?*)
A Halmstad ... Halmstad.
Q Bor du in i stan? (*Do you live in the town itself?*)
A På land. (*In the country.*)
Q På landet? a-a-a-a ... på en ... urrumph ... vad ... har du ... har ni ladugård? hästar? (*In the country? humph humph ... what ... have you* [singular] *... have you* [plural] *got a cowhouse? Horses?*)
A Uhuh. (*Yes.*)
Q Aha, så ni är bönder, då? (*So you're small farmers then?*)
A Uhuh. (*Yes.*)

An engraving of Halmstad in 1710 where Anna Karlsson says she comes from

Continuous Existences?

Q mhmhmh och vad heter du ? (... *and what is your name?*)

A Anna.

Q Anna ... vad då – det sista namnet ? (*Anna! what's the ... last name?*).

A Karlsson.

Q Ah. Anna Karlsson ?

A (*funny voice*) Trevligt att träffas. (*Pleased to meet you – or something stylized along these lines*)

The exchange is not particularly illuminating nor on the part of the subject in very good Swedish, but both fluency and thought seemed to be steadily improving as the short dialogue continued.

Mrs Isaacson's is one of those frustrating regressions in which it seems that a breakthrough is imminent and that the material is always just on the verge of yielding a definite answer to what is happening under hypnosis. But it never quite reaches that point, and is dogged by misfortune – the inadvertent 'Richmond', the fire at the army records office and the discovery of Anna Karlsson much too late to question her more fully and find out more about this new Swedish 'character'.

As always when looking at 'information' given in the lives, one is afraid of attaching too much importance to the half-truth when it may be only wishful thinking on the part of the observer: one hesitates to interpret the near-miss as a direct hit, and one is even cautious of trusting an indisputably correct fact as positive evidence when it may be only coincidence.

The most dramatic moments of the regressions, when Frances was genuinely incapable of understanding any language except Swedish, would seem to be most convincing had there not been recent Scandinavian ancestry. Mrs Isaacson is adamant that she does not speak the language but honestly adds that as a small baby she may have heard her mother and grandmother talking in Swedish. Of this, however, she has no conscious memory but it may lie buried in the unconscious just as a blind or deaf person who has had the use of eyes or ears for even a few weeks after birth is very different from one who was born without sight or hearing. Certainly the Swedish is not very good and often the answers are merely a repetition of a word or phrase in the question. The longest spontaneous and independent sentence (I am glad to meet you) could have been the greeting between her mother and grandmother, and the one that would impress itself on the uncomprehending mind of the baby Frances. Yet the fact remains that she was instantly able to understand everything that was asked her by a Swedish national speaking at normal conversational speed. Even if it is not supernatural, it is utterly staggering.

9. 'Gone but Not Forgotten'

Pat Roberts

Q Deep sleep ... deep sleep ... come forward six years ... it is now 1913. How are you Frances?

A (*feeble, querulous voice of an elderly person, obviously in pain*) I'm ... not ... well ... me leg ... me leg ... me leg ...

Q Come forward to the last moments of Frances Johnson (*repeated three times, punctuated with a faint 'Eh'? from the subject*)

A (*very weak indeed*) Want to know what he's doing here.

Q Who?

A Him in the black suit ... he's got a case.

Q Oh – he's the doctor.

A No ... he's got the papers ... John's papers ... (*pause, then in a flat, completely disinterested tone*) Oh – they're arranging the funeral.

Q Whose funeral?

A Mine … you've got to get these things arranged.

Q Not before you're dead, surely?

A (*almost inaudibly*) I told them to do it … I'm on me way out.

Q Whereabouts have you arranged to be buried? Somewhere nice?

A I'm going back … to where I belong.

Q Back to Bootle?

A I'm going back … home …

It is an eerie sensation to listen for many hours to Pat Roberts under deep hypnosis describing in detail the life of a Frances Jones who had flourished almost a century earlier and then to read in the parish register an entry for the burial of a person of that name and at the time given in the regression. It is even more chilling to read in the same register that on 22 July 1865 a Frederick Jones married a Frances Johnson. But the most macabre experience of all would have been to visit the churchyard of St Mary's, Bootle where, until it was destroyed by a chance German bomb in May 1941, there stood a headstone bearing the name Frances Jones, the date of death 17 September 1913, and ironically, or perhaps prophetically, the inscription *Gone but not forgotten.*

Pat Roberts, a twenty-seven-year-old former nurse now married to a doctor, came into regression almost accidentally, like so many of Keeton's subjects. She slipped into deep hypnosis very easily and began the long story that started with the five-year-old Frances Mary Rodrigues, born at 10 Bankfield Street, Bootle, about 1840, and ended two widowhoods and sixty-eight years later with the death of Frances Jones in Canning Street, Liver-

St Mary's Churchyard, Bootle. This is the graveyard in which Frances Jones was buried in 1913

pool. It is a convoluted account, full of strange aberrations and anachronisms, but all through there is a very significant framework of demonstrable facts of which Pat, at least in her conscious mind, has no knowledge. Perhaps the most remarkable of these is her use of names of people who are found to have existed at the time and place, if not in the relationship with one another that she describes. These are not the important citizens whose memorials might be seen today, but ordinary humble folk of the backstreets who are recorded nowhere but in the microfilm records of early street directories and municipal documents hidden away in library archives.

Pat's regressions often seem like the dreams in which the people and places and events have all been real enough but are hopelessly confused – you are married to a five-year-old whom you dimly remember from early school days, but she turns out to be your aunt: you live in London, which you know is really Edinburgh, and incidents you experienced at ten are now transposed to forty with a different cast and in a different place.

According to the 'biographical' facts that emerged under regression, Frances was born Frances Mary Rodrigues, some time before 1840, daughter of a cobbler of Spanish origin, Joe Rodrigues of 10 Bankfield Street, Bootle. Although not particularly prosperous, Joe seems to have had ambitions for his daughter and sent her to a girls' school run by a Mrs Van G ..., but withdrew her when she seemed incapable of learning to read. Frances was brought up fairly strictly but that did not prevent an early marriage about 1858–60 to an Alfred Johnson, master of the American-owned sailing ship *Franconia*. Alfred Johnson was said to have come from neighbouring Southport.

Widowed a few years later when the vessel sank off Anglesey, Frances Johnson married an accountant, Frederick Jones, who had been dealing with the papers of her late husband's ship and, as we have seen, a marriage between Frances Johnson and Frederick Jones did take place in 1865. Frederick appears to have died in the 1880s and now comfortably off and a confirmed hypochondriac, Frances Jones lived on – perhaps lingered on in the later years – until 1913. Again, as we have seen, a person of that name was buried in Bootle in September 1913.

Although Pat was not born in Bootle she did spend her childhood there, but as the tombstone of Mrs Jones had been destroyed ten years before Pat's birth there is no way in which she could have seen it. It seems beyond the bounds of possibility, too, that she could ever have seen the parish records of the marriage of Frederick and Frances Jones. If these and all the other names and incidents that crop up are the product of a mind running free under hypnosis then it seems that there must be more to coincidence than mere chance.

Pat is much more definite than most subjects in assuming the physical characteristics of the personality to which she has regressed, and her voice in particular has the tonal quality of early childhood, petulant adolescence, self-pitying unfulfilled middle age and quavering senility. At five she was crying with the typical sound of a small child in deep distress. She was in the

scullery, she said, because her mother had 'hit her round the ear' for sticking
her finger in the cake.

Q Did she put you in the scullery or did you go yourself?
A Went in by myself to cry. She told me to be quiet.
Q What does your father do, Frances?
A He mends shoes.

Fairly typically, she did not know whether he made or mended her own
shoes, or who lived next door – though she did know that there were no
neighbours on one side because it was not a proper house. In later regressions she said it was a warehouse, and indeed Bankfield Street today is almost
entirely warehouses. An attempt to get her full name was much more
successful, and the first real breakthrough came in this regression.

Q Do you know what your address is? The number on your door and the
  street?
A Got something to tell people if I get lost.
Q What is it?
A (*reciting in a sing-song, babyish voice*) Frances-Mary-Rodrigues-ten-Bankfield
  -Street-Bootle.

Frances had also said that her father's name was Joe, and with names and
addresses so positively identified – which is most unusual in a regression –
the first of the strange coincidences came to light. Pat's maternal grand-
father who died in 1964 was the natural son of a Spanish seaman, José
Rodriguez, who as far as is known never lived permanently in England but
who, when his ship was engaged in commerce in the port of Liverpool
found time for private and personal business in the city. Pat is adamant that
she had never heard anything like that name until it appeared on her tongue
under hypnosis and that the story of her great-grandfather came to light
only when she was talking to her mother about the regression. It could be
argued of course that she had quite unconsciously heard the name mentioned
as a very small baby when her mother had been discussing family history
with other adults and when she groped for a 'father' for the character she
had created, Joe (as an anglicized José) Rodrigues leaped from the unknown
depths of her mind.

On the other hand the street directories of Bootle state that a Joe
Rodrigues, a cobbler, did live at 10 Bankfield Street in the 1880s though it
has not been possible to trace him at that address any earlier. Early directories are notoriously unreliable, and householders of long standing are
liable to be omitted from an edition or two and then to reappear later at the
same address for no apparent reason. Joe Rodrigues may have been only a
lodger, or perhaps rented a room for a workshop earlier – Frances always
said that her father did his cobbling in the parlour and did not have a proper
shop. There were certainly Rodrigues in the district forty years before the

one mentioned in Bankfield Street – birth certificates for a George Frederick and an Elizabeth are in the registrar-general's records for 1841. Although the act requiring the registration of births and deaths was passed in 1837 it was not rigorously enforced until the 1870s, and a small town of only a few thousand people as Bootle was in the 1840s may well not have bothered with more than the entry in the parish register. If, as Frances maintained, Joe was a Catholic and did not have his children baptized in the Anglican church, there could well be no record at all.

At eight Franny, as she now called herself, was still very much the little girl with a facility for bursting into tears that seemed to indicate the over-indulged child who was well-practised in the use of weeping to gain her own ends.

Q Where are you Frances?
A In the yard.
Q What are you doing in the yard, Frances?
A (*sniff*) I'm … (*sniff*) … locked out. (*exploratory sobs, seeking sympathy*)
Q What are you doing? Playing with your dolly?
A Mum says … I'm (*savouring the word and playing to the gallery*) I'm con … tem
   … *platin'* [a common euphemism for going to the lavatory which would, of course, have been in the back yard]

The effect of the simpering precocity from the lips of the mature Pat was so incongruous that the observers spontaneously burst into laughter: immediately Frances, obviously furious that her ploy had not had the right response, howled with tears of rage and hurt pride.

When she had recovered her composure she began talking about her appearance – a subject which usually pleased her. Her hair, she said, was done in 'ringles' with paper that hurt, but when the word 'ringlets' was put to her, she brushed it aside imperiously. 'Ringles' she said emphatically. It would be interesting to know whether this was indeed a local term, or perhaps a purely personal one belonging to Frances – Pat says that she has no idea where it came from. Even if in these early sessions there had been an excellent recreation of the character of a small girl, there had been little definite factual material apart from the names. In the closing minutes of the sequence one more of these emerged, and it was felt that there must be something more than imagination at work.

Q What do you do? [i.e. in your spare time]
A Go and see Mrs Rafferty.
Q Where does she live?
A Down the road.
Q But where? In the same street as you live?
A (*silence*)
Q Why do you go to see her, Frances?
A They're old and me mum says it's nice to go and talk to them.

Q What do you talk about to Mrs Rafferty?
A She just talks and I sit there ... she tells me about Herbert ...

In her present life Pat knows no one of this name, but the street directories
show that a Mrs Raffert kept a boarding house in Denison Street in 1859 and
in Gibraltar Row three years later, though it does not indicate how long she
had been at the first address. Both streets are close to Bankfield Street in the
dock area of Bootle, and though the dates seem a little confused (Frances
would have been eight in the 1840s) it is an intriguing possibility.

At ten Frances is still immature but there are hints of the lines along which
her adult character will develop.

Q Have you ever been to school?
A Mmmm.
Q Where?
A Just to that ... lady ... don't like her.
Q What is her name?
A Mrs Van ... Van ... something. I don't know.
Q And where does she live?
A Don't know. Me dad takes me.
Q Do you walk?
A (shakes head) It was a long way. But I couldn't do me letters and I told me
   dad I didn't like it. He said I didn't have to go there anymore.
Q What do you want to do when you are big?
A (pause, then rolling the word round her mouth like an old-brandy connoisseur)
   Rich ... rich ...

Although Frances never achieved the full name of the school, she did
indicate in a later regression that it began with a 'G' sound, and again the
directories threw up their puzzling answer. A Mrs Elizabeth Van Gelder
ran a 'Ladies Seminary' at 28 Aigburth Street, near Smithdown Lane, about
the middle of the century. This would have meant a journey of about three
miles from Bankfield Street by the most direct route, and Frances did say it
was a long way. One can understand a father's reluctance, in view of distance
and fees, to let a daughter who was learning nothing continue with her
education.

For much of her regression to the teenage period Frances was questioned
by an expert in textiles and fashion from the Victoria & Albert Museum,
London, who concentrated on clothing and domestic matters. The history
of dress is of course a subject in which many women are interested so that
much of the detail has to be treated with caution as it could have come from
the conscious as well as the unconscious memory. There are some telling
points, however, which seem outside the scope of most readily-available
sources. At thirteen the girl feels the dignity of growing up and now insists
on being addressed as 'Frances' rather than 'Franny'. She wears a skirt –
indicating vaguely with her hand a mid-calf length – with a long-sleeved

linen top without a collar: for out of doors she has a shawl for warmth. All of this is relatively vague material which could apply over a long period of history, and is available in countless books and magazines and in thousands of hours of television drama. The 'leg' answers were however much more significant:

Q Does your father make your shoes?
A (*very definitely*) No.
Q Did you buy them?
A He bought them.
Q What colour are they?
A Red ... (*suddenly a childish delight in her voice*) red *bangy* shoes.
Q Bangy shoes? I have never heard of bangy shoes.
A When you walk they bang.
Q Ah – they have metal on the toes and heels?
A Mmmmm (*reluctantly admitting the fact*) They're ... clogs really.
Q Have you got stockings on?
A Yes – I've got stockings on.
Q How do you keep them up?
A (*surprised*) I just put my finger in them and twist them round.
Q You haven't got garters?
A No. Me dad won't let me wear them. He says they do something to your legs.

Again it would be interesting to know whether 'bangy shoes' was a personal and logical description of either Frances or Pat, or a contemporary colloquialism. Twisting the top of the stocking and then tying the loop in a knot or tucking it inside the tightened web was a childish trick practised in the nineteenth century and early-twentieth century still recalled by some elderly people whose parents, like Frances', believed that varicose veins and other dire conditions resulted from the constriction of garters. Pat insists that she had never heard of this, and that her conscious mind was completely puzzled by the meaning as the words tumbled out.

In general the routine domestic details were inconclusive. The family had porridge with salt and not milk for breakfast, and for the midday meal (Frances did not understand the word 'lunch' in the questioning and the conscious could be seen translating this to 'dinner') bread, cheese, onions and hot milk. The evening meal was 'all meat an' potatoes ... an' all mixed up ...' Frances rejected the word 'stew' and more surprisingly the classic Merseyside variation 'scouse' with which Pat must have been familiar since childhood.

Frances' claim to have eaten and enjoyed tomatoes was met with some scepticism as it was thought that these were not popular in England until towards the end of the century. Editions of Mrs Beeton in the early 1860s, however, list three recipes, though as the fruit seems to be unfamiliar she adds several notes on the background of 'The Tomato or Love Apple' which was widely considered to be poisonous at the time. It could be that if we are really listening to a daughter of Joe Rodrigues from Spain – where the tomato had been accepted for many years – the family could well have used it before it became popular.

Between the ages of fifteen and seventeen it was often as difficult to communicate with Frances as it would be with many young people today: she was in turn sulky, talkative, rude, evasive with far fewer spells of that co-operation and desire to please that seems characteristic of most subjects under hypnosis. Typical of this period are the following exchanges:

Q Do you ever go to New Brighton?
A (*resentfully and sullen*) Naaaaaoh. Never go anywhere.
Q What is the name of the ferry?
A Don' know ... can't read me letters.
Q What month is your birthday?
A (*long silence, and then obviously as a diversionary tactic begins to scratch her head violently*)
Q What are you scratching for?
A I 'aven't got fleas.
Q Have you got nits – there's nothing to be ashamed of ... everybody gets them.
A *I* don't ... me mum puts vinegar on me 'air ... (*as if sensing another question on these lines and wishing to change the subject, becomes full of self-pity*) Got ... spots ...

Later, in a more truculent mood and with the classic rebellion against parental standards:

Q It *is* your seventeenth birthday. What are you doing?
A Nuttin' at the moment.
Q 'Nuttin''? Your accent has altered. You used to speak very nicely. What's the matter?
A 'Snone of your business how I speaks.
Q It is. What did you have for your birthday?
A Tha's my business too, isn't it?

For her spots Frances said that her mother used to put on opium and chalk, but while this taken internally is a good old-fashioned remedy for settling the stomach, it seems unlikely that it would have done much good externally for acne. Washing, or at least rinsing the hair in vinegar was an ineffective folk remedy for head lice, but here, and later in Frances' life when symptoms and medication are a major part of her conversation, the material must be treated with caution because of Pat's own medical background.

Perhaps the most significant piece of material that emerged in the teenage sequence was the mention of a friend, Violet Langham, who was two years Frances' junior and whose father 'lifts boxes on the Exchange'. The two remain close friends throughout Frances' life, and it is Violet who is present at the last scene when the solicitor is arranging the funeral. In a much later session, Violet is described as having married, much against her will but under pressure from her parents, her cousin, Frederick Langham. The couple settled in Bootle, and the census returns do record that there was a Frederick Langdon, victualler, in Vauxhall Road in the 1880s.

Once again one of the strange coincidences that seem to underlie the whole of Frances' story occurred: a few days after the session in which Violet's marriage was mentioned Pat bought a miscellaneous collection of old books in a sale room, and on opening a family Bible which was among them she found a very old photograph of a lady, apparently in her thirties, and judging from the dress, taken about the turn of the century. On the back was written 'Merry Christmas, with love, from Violet'. A few months later Joe Keeton told Frances to open her eyes and holding the photograph in

The postcard of 'Violet' with its message on the back (*see margin*)

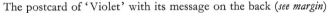

front of her asked if it was of her friend. Frances replied, 'it's like her, but too old … Violet's younger than that – she's younger than me'.

The period of Frances' twenties was an exciting one, full of material that seemed likely to check out and to give a breakthrough on the matter of regression. But slowly, as one tried to fit the various elements into place and into time, the whole began to slip away until one was left with a complex montage of people and events, but just as an unreal montage is made up of very real individual elements, so is Frances' story. There was a short romance with Alfred Johnson from neighbouring Southport, who was first mate on the sailing ship *Franconia* and who had come into her father's shop for shoe repairs. A ship of this name was on the Liverpool–America run in the first half of the century: she was of 510 tons fully rigged and built at Medford, Massachusetts, in 1834. Carrying a general cargo, mainly tobacco, she was wrecked off Anglesey in January 1851 with a loss of all her crew –the date presents a major problem, because by her own reckoning Frances would have been only eleven when her husband to whom she had been married for several years was drowned. There is obviously something wrong, yet Frances gave clearly under regression the name of the ship, the fact that it was American-owned, and that she was wrecked off Anglesey. In an attempt to resolve the difficulties she was asked about the wedding, but was most reluctant to volunteer even a vague date.

One other detail of the marriage was interesting though.

Q Where were you married?
A In Bootle.
Q Where about in Bootle?
A The little relief church …

No one could trace any record of an establishment of that name, but eventually the borough librarian who had been working on the question said that it could well be an early, or alternative, name for the church of St Mary, Bootle. For a long time it was the only church in the growing town, and had been built in 1827 as a chapel of ease to relieve the over-crowded congregations at St Mary's, Walton-on-the-Hill. The description 'little relief' is not one which any imagination would apply to a church normally unless there was some very special reason for doing so, and this strange reference is most significant.

Names of people seem the strongest element in Pat's regression: in a later regression she was picked up waiting at the docks for her husband to return.

Q Any sign of your husband yet? Where are you going to meet him?
A If he doesn't hurry up I'm going to the coffee house. It's at the pier.
Q You're going to the coffee house? Where did you say you were meeting him?
A At the Customs House.
Q Now tell me, can you describe this hackney carriage you were looking at?

What colour is the horse?

A *(very emphatically) Two horses.*

Q [Questioner was obviously thinking of the hansom cab which was later to become universal in cities] I didn't know hackney carriages had TWO horses.

A *This* one's got *two* ...

There is no coffee house at the Pier today, but in the mid-nineteenth century, The Merchants' Coffee House, licensed to sell beer and spirits stood next to St Nicholas's Church by St George's Dock which is only a short step from the Customs House. It was a popular meeting place for seamen and their families, but was closed in 1883, leaving no trace except in the archives – an area with which Pat is most unfamiliar. If it was the twentieth-century Pat speaking, she would be more likely to use 'coffee bar' or 'coffee shop' than 'coffee house'.

The force with which Frances rejected the one-horse hackney is unusual as subjects so often change their answer when they suspect that the questioner thinks they have given an incorrect one. The hackney did, of course, have two horses. In her waking state Pat, whose experience of regression is to watch the scene, including herself, as if she was looking at a cinema screen, says that the two horses were very real and that it almost annoyed her to be contradicted when she could see them in front of her.

As in real life, when one is weary of waiting, conversation began to languish, and *à propos* of nothing someone asked:

Q Tell me, is there an overhead railway?

A *(immediately, excited)* The Dingle ... Seaforth ... The Dockers' Umbrella ...

Q That's right ... have you been on it?

A *(very excited) Yes ... I have (pause)* It' s a bit ricketty, isn't it?

Q Yes.

A *(suddenly, and most unusual for a subject under regression, Frances sings)* On the ... Din ... gle ... Sea ... forth Overhead ... Line ... th'Overhead ... Line ... – that's a song, you know ...

If such a song did exist, it has not been traced, but the sequence is important. A Frances Jones who died in 1913 would naturally have been aware of the Dingle to Seaforth line, which was nicknamed the Dockers' Umbrella, but as this was opened for general operation in the 1880s, Frances Johnson in the 1860s could not have known of it. However, as so many small points which at first seemed incorrect had been found to be right, the subject was thought to be worth further investigation – and it was discovered that a section of the Yorkshire and Cheshire from Sandhills to the docks was opened in 1855 and on the quay section ran some six metres above ground level on iron supports. It was originally intended to speed up the transport of coal from Wigan to the sea, but was soon popular as a passenger line. Did a Frances Johnson travel on this elevated track in the 1860s – in a later

The Dingle-Seaforth Railway soon after its opening

regression she said it was only a very short stretch – or did a Frances Jones travel later in the century on the better-known Dingle-Seaforth line and confuse the dates? Or did Pat Roberts ride the train in the second half of the century before it was demolished in 1958 – certainly it ran through Bootle where she was brought up. Once more, one feels so close to an answer, and then the whole picture mists over so that little can be seen.

Taken at random to the age of twenty-eight, Frances became deeply distressed and eventually said that Alfred was missing. She said that a man had just been to see her.

Q Did he say what happened?
A No wreckage.
Q Did he say they were absolutely sure?
A No ... he said it's three months now ...
Q Have they kept paying you?
A Just brought me some now.
Q How much has he brought you?
A Twelve guineas ...

At this point she broke down and could say no more: brought forward another year (twenty-nine) she was more composed and answered instantly.

Q Have you been to the shipping company to see what has happened? If they are going to pay you a pension? What about the ship's certificates and that sort of thing?
A Well ... I went to Dale Street [one of the main commercial streets in Liverpool] y'see ... to see [word unintelligible] for this certificate ...

Q Who was that?
A Mr Jones.
Q How are you making your money now?
A Well ... Alfred had a ... few things ... lodged with Mr Jones ... you see.
And Mr Jones does something with the bankers ... and I've got to go
down every Wednesday afternoon to pick up me money.
Q How much do they give you?
A Thirty shillings ... and six pence a week.

There were hints that an attachment was developing between Frances and
Mr Jones, and then suddenly she had married him. In all of the regressions
to her second marriage she always refers to her husband as ' John' but says
that this is her personal name for him – he is really Frederick. The dating is
always imprecise: on one occasion she says definitely that she married
Alfred Johnson in 1862, and then on another:

Q How long have you been married? [to Johnson, that is]
A Four years.
Q What year would that be?
A Don't know.
Q Have there been any exciting occasions in the last year or two that you
have enjoyed?
A Silver Jubilee ... party in the street ... and bunting.

As Queen Victoria's Silver Jubilee was in 1862, her first marriage must have
been before 1858.

The marriage certificate from St Mary's, Bootle, which was discovered
only some time after Frances Johnson had described her marriage to
Frederick Jones, is almost a nightmare in which all the components merge
into weird and unexpected combinations. The whole thing seems like one of
those optical illusions that seem now a vase, now two faces, now something
else. The only facts which correspond with the regression are Frances' age
and address, and Frederick's condition as a widower. Frances (whose middle
name becomes Taylor and not Mary) is described as a spinster, and her
father an accountant; a Giles Johnson is shown in a directory of 1847 as a
book-keeper in Derby Road, Bootle, but had obviously assumed a grander
title by the time of his daughter's marriage. Frederick Moreton Jones
appears to be a printer from Southport (the home of Alfred Johnson) but
his father was a shoemaker named John. It is interesting to note that this
Frances Johnson could write – at least enough to sign her name, though she
does this with what was, even then, the old-fashioned 'f'-shaped terminal
's' and with what seems a very unaccustomed hand.

Checking this material for the regression is made difficult because so
much of the material from Merseyside – buildings, streets, and documents –
was destroyed in the air raids of the Second World War: Bootle itself is said
to have been the most intensely bombed borough of Britain, with more than

The entry in the Bootle Parish Register recording the marriage of Frederick Jones and Frances Johnson

ninety per cent of its homes damaged or destroyed. Although the church of St Mary was reduced to rubble its registers were saved, but unfortunately the fuller details of the death of Frances Johnson cannot be traced at the Office of Population, Censuses and Surveys in London. While in the Registrar-General's department where millions of names are being dealt with annually there must be mistakes, accidents and omissions, the chances of both the certificates important to this regression being lost must be very remote, and we seem confronted with yet another of the coincidences that are associated with this case history.

As the wife and widow of Frederick Jones, Frances did not produce much that could be checked historically. She was largely concerned with petulant grievances during his life and with her own ailments after his death. Much of the dialogue from this period could rise from imagination because there are so few positive facts to fasten it to the framework of reality.

Q How are things with you, Frances?
A (*reluctantly*) All right.
Q How is your husband?
A As right as he ever will be ...

On another occasion after a catalogue of the symptoms of her 'bronchial spasms' for which her doctor prescribed an inhaler:

Q How is your husband now?
A Uh ... just as ever ... it's ... of ...
Q Has he still got his gout?
A Yeh ... an' he's got his big red nose ... bald ... 's bad breath ... he's
terrible ... I'm hiding in the attic ... I couldn't stand him today ... NO.

Frances says that she spends much of her time crocheting doileys, which
she gives away, and entertains her husband's visitors in the rigid social
stratification of Victorian England. She feels she is not accepted as belonging
to their class.

Q Now that you have married into what is effectively a rich family, are you
moving in different circles?
A Trying to.
Q What about big societies ... or ladies' groups?
A No – I'm not accepted.
Q Because of your accent?
A Mmmm ... and my sallow skin [This reference to her complexion derived
from her Spanish ancestry keeps occurring]
Q Does that anger you?
A They can take me or leave me ... I couldn't give a bugger ...

If the Frances here is the Frances Rodrigues, daughter of a humble cobbler,
the diatribe is understandable: if it is the memory of Frances Taylor
Johnson, daughter of the accountant who married the son of a shoemaker,
it is difficult to see the reasoning behind it. Even if as a printer – and he
appears in later directories as a bookseller – he had been successful, Frederick
Johnson would not have been accepted by the best society because he was
'in trade'. Could there have been a mistake, either deliberate or accidental in
the parish register? The existence of a Giles Johnson, be he book-keeper or
accountant, makes this difficult to believe. Or does the social ostracism
sequence spring from the depths of Pat's own mind? She readily admits
that her own background is 'working class'. By her own efforts she has
made a good professional career for herself and has married a doctor. Does
there still exist somewhere deep in her unconscious mind a fear – quite un-
founded in today's climate – that she herself might not be fully accepted?

Much of this part of Frances' regression concerns health and although the
symptoms of acute arthritis, chest pains and later the general failing of her
faculties are given with accuracy, as were the remedies which would have
been used at the time, because she has a medical background not as much
weight can be given to them as could be if she were a layman. Nevertheless,
the way in which she felt and re-enacted the symptoms was very impressive
– after a regression Pat experienced for several days the pain in the knee
joints which, in Frances, were the most affected areas.

There are a few details from this period which have more relevance in
trying to establish some historical authenticity.

Q What about the dress shops in Liverpool, Frances? Are there any nice shops where I can buy a coat or gown?

A You're better having it made, I think.

Q Where do you suggest I go?

A I get my fabrics from ... McGinty's ... in Everton Brow ... up by the old church ...

It has not been possible to trace a McGinty's, but there was a McGinlays tailors shop in a now-vanished Palm Street in the 1860s. It may be significant that at the time of the regression a song called 'McGinty's Goat' had some popularity: Pat was certainly aware of it, and it could be that her unconscious, groping for a name that would not come clearly, was prompted by her conscious with the nearest word it could supply.

Q But suppose I want to look at the shops in town. Do you know a place called Bon Marché?

A (*instantly*) Bon Marché – that's in Church Street ... on the corner ... by Parker Street ... They have Paris stuff in there.

Q Is it expensive? What would I have to pay for a day gown?

A Depends on how many petticoats and things you want to go with it. A nice one ... reasonable ... say two guineas.

Q What about a pair of gloves?

A Oh ... about ten bob.

Q And a pair of boots?

A About twenty-five bob.

Bon Marché, the up-market branch of Lewis's which certainly did feature Paris fashions, was opened in Church Street, Liverpool, near the Parker Street corner in 1877. Unfortunately it was taken over in 1961 so that there is a chance that Pat may have been aware of it as a child. The prices she quotes seem to fall in the lower-middle-class range for this period.

Frances claimed that she and her husband lived in the 'posh' area of Canning Street, though she would not say which number. Much of this street of imposing Victorian houses for well-to-do businessmen still stands, and though many of the buildings have now come down in the social scale by being divided into flats, there is no mistaking that it was once a prosperous locality, even if there is a hint of the nouveau riche about it. It was presumably in the early days at Canning Street that the following took place:

Q Where *are* you living these days?

A Canning Street.

Q What number are you?

A Ah ... um (*struggles to remember, and mutters to herself*) I don't know the number I'm in ... it's next door to Mr Ellenbogen.

Q Is he a surgeon?

A No – he's a merchant.

The street directories do not list a Mr Ellenbogen in Canning Street, but in the 1880s there was an Isaac Ellenbogen, glass merchant, in Crown Street only a short distance away. Pat is adamant that she has never consciously met the very unusual surname Ellenbogen, so that its use here seems to imply that something beyond chance or imagination is at work.

There is less ambiguity about the next reference to Canning Street: though the exact date was not established it seemed that in the early 1880s, Frances' husband had been dead almost a year, and she said 'I have three more weeks of the black'.

Q What are you going to do now? Look for another husband?
A No ... *no* ... I'm not going to do that.
Q Shall you move house?
A I've thought about that, but I'll stay in the same area.

In the 1870s there is a Frances Jones at 32 Canning Street – she has no husband, but has two sons – John, a book-keeper (accountant) and Willie, a shipping clerk. There is also a John Jones, gentleman, at no. 149. Most remarkable of all is Mrs Frances Jones who in 1881 was living at no. 165 and not far away at no. 148 John William Jones, accountant: is the Frances Jones who was now at no. 32 in the 1870s (whose antecedents do not seem to tie up with the Rodrigues line) the same one who was at no. 165 in the

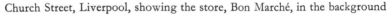

Church Street, Liverpool, showing the store, Bon Marché, in the background

next decade? Just who was who, and if Pat Roberts was neither, how did
the strange comment that she had moved at the correct period come into her
head?

Canning Street had two more significant episodes before the four walls of
Frances' bedroom closed like a prison round her, her swollen ankles, her
red and shining knee joints, wheezing chest, her hard, dry cough, her per-
petual complaints and her commode. Monica O'Hara, a Liverpool journalist
who some weeks earlier had interviewed a life-long resident of the street
who was then in her eighties, asked:

Q Have you come across an old vagrant ... an old lady in rags ... who
   knocks on doors? Has she ever knocked on your door?
A She doesn't *sell* rags ... she asked for them ... she's a poor soul.

For the next half-dozen questions relating to the old beggar Frances was
completely silent, but her forehead wrinkled as if she was puzzling to
remember something. Then suddenly she burst out, ignoring the last
question she had been asked: '*They call her Biddy Costello*'. When Monica
O'Hara checked, the old lady confirmed that the vagrant's name had indeed
been Biddy Costello.

Towards the end of her life Frances was complaining of the pain in her
chest, obviously some heart condition.

Q Does the doctor come to see you about it?
A Only old Doctor Rigby.
Q Does he use a stethoscope on your chest?
A (*does not understand – mumbles Mmmmm but it does not signify yes*).
Q Does he give you anything for it?
A He gives me digitalis ... and I take laudanum ...

The directories do list a Dr George Owen Rigby, physician and surgeon, at
51 Shaw Street in the mid 1890s, but there is no trace in the records of a Dr
Buchan who Frances mentions more frequently.

In the bursting world at the turn of the century these seem trifling events
to remember when the only occasions of national significance that Frances
can remember – and then only very vaguely – are the Golden and Diamond
Jubilees and the war in South Africa. But living in an age of radio and television perhaps we cannot realize just how limited life must have been to a
bedridden old woman whose only communication with the outside was
through the frail, elderly and now widowed Violet Langham who, Frances
claims, was looking after her.

Communicating with Frances in her later years was difficult because of
deafness, and question after question had to be repeated. In one session she
had indicated that the year was 1913.

Q How are you today, Frances? (*repeated more loudly*)

A (*Pause, then wearily*) Weight on my chest ... so heavy ... Have to sit up in bed. *Oh ... Oh ... my leg ...*

The voice became weaker and weaker, and to make themselves heard the questioners had to shout quite loudly: Frances appeared to be dying and was brought to her last memories:

A I'm going back ... to where I belong ... I don't care where they put me ... but it must be home ... in Bootle ... I'll rest ... easy there.
Q Is your brother with you?
A No ... I've not heard from him for years ... Edward's gone ... and now ... I'm ... going ... home.

The breathing became laboured, there was a deep groan, and Pat's head slumped to one side: Frances Jones, whoever she may have been, had gone.

As we have seen a Frances Jones was buried in Bootle in September 1913 – but unfortunately this cannot be the alleged Frances-Rodrigues-Johnson-Jones of the regression as the lady in grave number 91, St Mary's Churchyard was the wife of an Edward Jones, sawyer, of Bibby Lane, Bootle. The sheer complexity and confusion of Pat Robert's story makes even a suggested explanation very difficult, yet striding through the whole regression are the disturbingly accurate names, Rodrigues, Frances Johnson, Frances Jones, Ellenbogen, Rigby, Biddy Costello, Langham, Rafferty, *Franconia*, 10 Bankfield Street, Canning Street, Merchant's Coffee House and St Mary's Churchyard – all of them at the right time and place, but most of them in a curious way just a little off the mark. To pull by chance two or three of them from imagination might be acceptable as coincidence but the consistency seems to indicate that it cannot be entirely the workings of a mind flicking through its unconscious memory to weave a story.

While some of the marginal incidents may reflect the hopes and fears of Pat's conscious mind it seems unlikely that the main account can ever have been part of memories of this life which she has forgotten – the documentary sources are too obscure, too diverse and too uninteresting for her ever to have come across them. The bizarre intertwining of two personalities of the same name, as well as the Rodrigues element which could well be quite separate, all living at approximately the same time seems inconsistent with reincarnation as we imagine it to be. On the basis of the material as it stands the only explanation – and that very unconvincing – is that some part of Pat's mind is dipping at random, yet in a strangely selective way, into a great pool of impersonal knowledge. But all the time one feels that there is a vital element missing. What this element might be is almost as difficult to imagine as the answer to regression itself: one can only hope that in a later session someone will ask the question that links in a logical way the lives of two – or three – ladies who have been dead for almost three-quarters of a century.

Epilogue

Are we, searching for an explanation of the phenomenon of regression, being offered the accepted but incorrect explanations, while the real one, unsuspected, is staring us in the face? Does the real answer to regression lie in the explanations suggested here, or is it beyond the limits of the human mind? It is said that if a two-dimensional creature were placed on the inside of a sphere it would have to move all round the inner surface to get to the opposite side because there is no way in which it could conceive the existence of a diameter, as we can with our three-dimensional outlook.

Are we trying to do something which will for ever be impossible in the light of our present knowledge, like travelling beyond the speed of light? Or are we groping slowly towards the truth, and when we have reached it be utterly amazed that we could not see it before? Or do we really see it now, but most of us refuse to accept it wholly because of what someone once described as 'the clockwork mind that Newton wound up three centuries ago'?

Perhaps the opening moments of a bizarre regression by a young policeman is on the right lines. The whole was spoken in a flat, mechanical voice that sounded as if it had come from a machine or else from a newly raised corpse in a horror film:

Q What are you doing?
A *I ... am ... me ... who ... are ... you?*
Q I'm Joe. What is your name?
A *I ... am ... me. I cannot ... see ... you. Where ... are ... you?*
Q I am around with you.
A *Why ... are ... you ... hiding? You cannot stop me ... I do not care who you are.*
Q Where *are* you going?
A *You ... cannot ... stop ... me.*
Q No – we do not want to stop you ... we want to come with you ... we are going the same way.

Index

Characters 're-lived' during regressions are shown in inverted commas. Page references in *italic* type indicate illustrations.